IT'S NOT COMMON CENT$

A 30-DAY PERSONAL FINANCE CRASH COURSE FOR COLLEGE STUDENTS AND YOUNG ADULTS: HOW TO MANAGE MONEY, SAVE MONEY FAST, PAY OFF DEBT AND INVEST IN THE STOCK MARKET

AAMINAH AMIN

CONTENTS

To my incredible husband, who has loved me and supported me no matter what.

To my amazing parents, who believed in me when I didn't believe in myself. Thank you for everything.

MONEY MASTERY STARTER KIT:
5 POWERFUL TOOLS TO ACCELERATE YOUR JOURNEY TO FINANCIAL FREEDOM

In your Money Mastery Starter Kit, you'll gain access to:

- An unconventional step-by-step guide to getting your finances under control
- A life-changing method for understanding and transforming your spending habits
- A detailed spending plan to set your financial goals for the next 12 months
- A budget tracker that makes tracking money easy AND fun
- A priceless tool for tracking your financial progress

Download Your FREE Copy Now! Visit www.30daymoneyschool.com OR scan the QR code with your phone:

INTRODUCTION

"Those who don't manage their money will always work for those who do".

— DAVE RAMSEY

Look at that Dave Ramsey quote again. Man, what a wake-up call to learn how to fix your finances!

Is Ramsey right, though? Robert Kiyosaki (1998), author of *Rich Dad Poor Dad*, one of the best-selling personal finance books of all time, agrees:

"Money is one form of power. But what is more powerful is financial education. Money comes and goes, but if you have

the education about how money works, you gain power over it and can begin building wealth. The reason positive thinking alone does not work is because most people went to school and never learned how money works, so they spend their lives working for money" (19).

School doesn't teach this stuff. It tends to stick with the tried and tested model of complex algebraic equations, integration, and quadratics. Did you notice the word *tried?* It's an anagram of *tired.* Alright, I'll concede that for some professions it has some use, but let's be honest, not that much. Heck, I've worked in big finance for years, and I've yet to be tested on anything that plus, minus, multiply, and divide couldn't solve.

You know what they say—the best time to plant a tree is 30 years ago; the second best time is now. And so it is with all this numbers and finance malarkey. Not the boring stuff like taxes or how the government runs the economy. Just basic knowledge like how credit cards work, what a retirement account is, and how investments work. Oh, geez, my eyes are glazing over just writing that. Let's see if I can make it easier.

Let's start at the very beginning, a very good place to start (small nod to *The Sound of Music*). Wait, you haven't watched it? Are you kidding me? Right—if you want to learn about personal finance you need to watch *The Sound of Music*. No, it's got nothing to do with money actually; it's just a great movie.

Let's go back to that basic knowledge we were talking about, like how the plastic in your wallet or purse gives you money that isn't yours so you can buy things you don't need with money you don't have. Then it charges you an arm and a leg for that dubious pleasure. That's credit cards.

Or what about the big pot of money they hand over to you when you hit the big six-five, or whatever the age is in your country when they think you've done enough and let you walk away from paid employment into the often uncomfortable arms of retirement. The tax man smiles and takes his cut, health insurance costs spiral upward, and the kids who never learned better still come by to visit the Bank of Mom and Dad. It turns out that big pot of money wasn't that big after all. And you're living longer, so by the end, you'll be scraping the bottom of that barrel. That's a retirement account.

Sometimes you should cross the road, and sometimes you should wait because cars are still coming at you. That's known as risk, and when it comes to your money, crossing the road or waiting is known as investing or delaying investing. When you avoid all hurtling vehicles and cross the road safely, with money we call that 'reward'. Because crossing the road is taught correctly, you know to look right and left and cross at the right time. Your parents taught you that and your teachers at school reinforced it. As for your friends—well, they help you remember this should you (on that extremely rare occasion) become rather the worse for wear and head blindly for the freeway in, shall we say, not a straight line. None of us want to be scraping you off the asphalt. Shouldn't the same concern be there for your finances?

But this they do not teach, even in the finest universities and colleges. Then again, why would they? Undergraduates pay exorbitant fees for the privilege of receiving a piece of paper. If they could truly work out risk and reward, they might dig a little deeper and decide against the financial millstone a college education hangs around their necks.

Harvard University, bless its heart, does offer students an annual personal finance workshop (Carpenter, 2019). The fourth module in the last workshop is called "Behavioral & Cognitive Issues in Personal Finance" (Harvard University). Right. Where do I sign up? I need some extra sleep. And because personal finance education is so rare, even this meek effort is lauded as a step forward. Well done, Harvard. Princeton hosts a financial literacy day because, as everyone knows, $1.4 trillion problems can be solved in a day. (Incidentally, $1.4 trillion is what 44 million Americans owe in student loan debt (Bolton, 2020).

If you're like me, chances are no one taught you any of these things. In fact, your first introduction to health insurance premiums might have occurred when you graduated from college! "What are health insurance premiums?" you ask. I know you know what they are, but I'm having fun writing this, so let's call them the few dollops of dosh you pay out to some shadowy Great Benefit company (yes, I'm referencing the 1997 movie *Rainmaker* with Matt Damon there) in the hope that when you get sick, they'll hand over many more dollops to the hospital charged with your care. None of us can afford to pay the actual costs of the hospital—they are far too high—so insurance companies take a little bit of money from a lot of people and say they'll cover their medical bills. (Side note: It's quite normal that the little bit they take increases regularly, and the percentage of your bill they cover decreases just as regularly.) Then the insurance company hopes like crazy that they only need to pay the large medical bills of a few of those people. They're also looking at risk, and when you apply for coverage, they're thinking, "We only want healthy people who give us lots of money and don't cost us much. We don't want sick people or people who will probably get sick later. Let our competitors look after them."

You're not the only one who hasn't been educated about these things. This is not an accident. While the economy has had its ups and downs and the wealth gap between the 1% and the rest of the population has increased, blaming everything on external factors is unfair. At the heart of this problem is America's terrible record with financial education.

If you've yearned for real financial education, it's likely the Internet has been a key resource. That's better than nothing. There are great sites out there such as Investopedia and Nerd-Wallet, but none of those websites address the real issue. Most people visiting those websites don't know anything about money. I'm not talking about how money works or its role in the economic system. Those are abstract ideas that won't help you save and grow your money or plan for a comfortable retirement. I'm talking about understanding how to make money work for you, about how you need cash flow and why that is different from your net worth.

Money is not a complex topic. You can add, right? You can use brackets and so on. Not hard. It can be intimidating, though, when all of it is thrown at you all at once. So I promise to only throw small bits at you and wait long enough between throws to let you catch the last bit, stuff it in your mouth, and swallow it. When I began my personal finance education journey, it was a challenge to sift through all the noise and so many complicated sounding words. And you know what? Underneath all the seeming complexity, I found some really simple building blocks and some blindingly easy concepts. Think of Legos for a moment. The pieces aren't complicated, and any age group can make models with them. Once you understand the basics, you can build models from simple all the way up to 100,000+ piece artworks you see at Legoland. So it is with personal finance. This book shows you the really simple building blocks of money and the blindingly easy concepts for how to manage it. You'll learn these concepts quickly—they're really not hard—and then it's up to you where you go from there.

I made it out of the noise and chaos, and so can you (with my help, of course). I keep my finances tidy and uncomplicated since I prefer quick to manage over lots to manage. You'll make your own decisions in time.

FINANCE VS. PERSONAL FINANCE

It wasn't that long ago that I was a fresh-faced university graduate looking to make my mark on the world. I graduated from a prestigious college and landed a good job in the financial sector in the United Kingdom. Since I was hired to work in finance, I obviously knew a lot about money, right? Nope. Not a chance. I knew about numbers. My job was in risk management, and numbers are the way we work out risk. But money? I didn't have a clue. My credit cards were maxed out, and I had taken out student loans to pay for an overpriced education that I hardly ever used day-to-day.

At the time, I didn't see this as a problem. I figured it was normal to borrow money from credit cards. Scratch that. I didn't even know that delaying repayment for things bought on a credit card meant I was borrowing money. I thought it all magically sorted itself out. Then there was my student loan debt. This was an "investment," I thought. When anyone asked me about it, I parroted the line that it was an investment in my future and that it was this debt that had gotten me my job.

People who apply to be the proper black-cab taxi drivers for the City of London have to pass a ridiculously intense exam that tests their intricate knowledge of the city's roads and neighborhoods. They have to describe how to get from A to B from memory and without a satellite navigation system. If you know anything about London, you know how hard that is. You'd think working in finance would require the same level of specialized knowledge. After all, it's people's money we're looking after. The answer to that is *No, it doesn't.*

To keep going with the taxi driving example, if you can drive a car and have a generally decent sense of direction, you're hired. In finance it's more: if you can work accurately, know numbers and get on with people, you'll be just fine. Like me. And if you know anything about Microsoft Office, you'll be seen as a genius. There's your handy tip of the day—if you want people to think you're smart, learn how to use Microsoft Office and go work in finance.

It took me a while to put things together, but once I began connecting the dots, I realized I was walking around with a ball and chain tied to my ankles. How could I expect to rise in life with such a burden? I began consuming everything related to personal finance and spoke to knowledgeable colleagues. I was lucky enough to be in close contact with financial advisors and other people who knew how money worked. Slowly but surely, my financial situation began to improve, and I'm now proudly debt-free.

I've studied personal finance for over five years and have applied all of the principles you'll learn in this book. What made the biggest difference for me was adopting a plan that was time-bound. This is my intention in giving you a 30-day plan. It is actionable, and it gives you clear steps to take. (Don't forget that the first step is to watch *The Sound of Music* if you haven't already.)

Study the information in this book at your own pace. I said I'd throw only small bits at you, but the reality is that I'm tossing the whole book at you and trusting that you will bite off what you can realistically chew. Read a chapter a week, and have an action plan for the following week at the very least. If you can manage more, do so. I've shot the lofty jargon out of the sky for you and kept it to the bare minimum. Truth be told, to master your finances, you need to learn a few complicated sounding words. Instead of focusing on the words themselves, we'll learn the lesson and then put a word to it.

I've provided as many analogies and examples as possible to help you easily understand the topics. We'll cover everything from budgeting to investing to creating income streams. All the advice in this book is tried and tested, so it's not as if you're being asked to build a castle in the sky. All the advice is practical, and best of all, you can implement it right away!

Can you get rid of all your financial problems in 30 days? No. Of course not. The 30 days refers to giving you an education that puts you on the right track. Then you'll practice, and with practice comes mastery. How long it takes to sort out your finances will depend on how dedicated you are to learning and applying the contents of this book.

You wouldn't take a long journey down the interstate in a car with wobbly wheels, a busted engine, and dodgy brakes. You'd be okay with less serious problems such as worn leather seats or dents in the bodywork. But if that car is about to explode and send you careening off the road into a ditch, it needs to get fixed. Pronto.

If your finances are like that car, by the end of 30 days, you'll learn how to fix those wobbly wheels, diagnose the engine problems, and replace the failing brakes. Over time, with consistent action, you'll fix problems bit by bit, and one day, you'll have a smooth and reliable roadster that will take you wherever you want to go. Better seats and no dents would be nice as well, and maybe that will happen in time.

Great results don't happen overnight, which is why consistency is important. The advantage of having a timeline is that it enforces discipline. You have something to do every day. This reinforces your intention to create good financial habits, which are the key to success. When you couple them with desire, you'll reach your goals even faster than you thought.

To totally misquote another great movie, the BAFTA-award-winning *Baby Driver*, "*Sometimes all I want to do is head west on 20 in a car I've fully paid off with a clear and concise plan. Just me, my music, the road, and my finances in order."* The real quote has the complete opposite meaning, so let's move on real quick before anyone spots the truth.

What we're about to get into is all straightforward and full of common sense. All you need is the right person to teach you, and I've got your back. So let's do this!

I

BEFORE WE GET INTO THE NITTY GRITTY

1

FINANCIAL JARGON – ONLY WHAT YOU NEED TO KNOW

We're going to learn 10 financial jargon terms. Getting these under your belt now will help your learning, and from that learning will come better financial decisions. Like those Lego models we talked about earlier, you can do a lot with 10 basic pieces. Most people don't know these terms, and if you're one of the few who do, that's awesome. For the rest of you, remember them throughout this 30-day crash course. I will use them *a lot*.

You do not need to sit down or brace yourself for this section. It's not hard, and I promise it will not be painful. The pain comes later (cue scary, malevolent, echoing laughter on the audio book soundtrack). Are you completely terrified? Nah, don't be. I'll make it easy for you. Let's get started.

You go out for drinks with a few friends. Each person buys a round of drinks for the others. Several rounds in, it's your turn. As the bartender brings the drinks, you realize with embarrassment that you left your money at home. You lean over to your best friend and whisper, "Lend me $50? I'll pay you back tomorrow. Left my money at home." He laughs as he hands the cash over, and you know you'll be ribbed about it later, but that's better than the alternative of confessing your mistake in front of everyone. The next day you pay him back and thank him for helping you out of a jam. If you want to know the jargon, that $50, the amount you borrowed from your decent and honest friend, is the **principal (Jargon #1)**. It's not the guy who ran your high school (he was one creepy dude), although the spelling is the same.

Check you out! Jargon # 1—nailed it! Principal! All the money you borrow. Nice job.

Let's revisit last night's drinks scenario with a few changes. Your best friend wasn't there, so when you discovered your money was at home, you realized the person next to you was a friend but not such a good one (and in a while will be even less of a good one). That's because as he hands over the $50, he whispers back, "I'm saving your ass, so I want $55 back tomorrow." You still don't want to lose face in front of the rest of the crowd, so you take his money. The next day you give him back—what was the name of that original amount? Yup, you got it. The principal. But you carry on forlornly about the extra $5, still holding it in your hand. "Are you really sure you want this, too?" you ask him. You're thinking about the lunch you need to buy and now can't. "Absolutely," he says and whips it out of your hands. He bows sarcastically and jogs off. So that extra $5, the money you paid back over and above the principal, is (jargon time) **interest (Jargon #2)**. Interesting, huh? And here *is* an interesting point about interest (okay, semi-interesting). It comes all the way from the Medieval Latin word *interesse*, which means "compensation for loss."

If you think about that, it makes sense. When you borrowed the principal that person stood to lose the money he lent you because you might not have given it back. When it was your best friend, he didn't want compensation for loaning you that money—after all, he's your friend. But when the scenario changed and it wasn't your best friend anymore, he did want compensation, so he charged you interest. He wanted more than what he gave you as compensation for possibly losing it all.

You've just learned Jargon #2. Interest! It's what you have to pay back over and above the principal. You're rocking this!

Let's step it up a notch because you've got this.

Instead of borrowing a principal of $50 from a friend, let's imagine you want to buy a car. It's a bit more expensive than a round of drinks, so you can't approach a friend to lend you the money. Your tastes are modest, so you're going for a popular, reasonable car, the Nissan Altima. You've found a good deal on a second-hand one, a 2019 model with only 8,000 miles on the odometer. The price is $17,500. You've got a sneaky $2,000 sitting in your bank account, so you decide to take it out and pay part of that $17,500 right away. That $2,000 is called the **down payment (#3)**. Ding ding! That's Jargon #3. I was going to give you the Latin for this word as well, but then I decided one per book is enough. You can look it up if you want (after you've watched *The Sound of Music*).

Moving swiftly on in the same imaginary situation, now you're at the car dealership having a good chat with the sales guy. There's a bit of flirting, if that's your thing, chatting about football ("Just how good is Odell Beckham Jr.!"), whatever it might be. The sales guy explains everything you need to know and then, glancing around, says, "Listen, I shouldn't be doing this, but I'm going to knock $500 off the price, just because I like you and I think it could help." Fist bump! You've just earned yourself a **discount (Jargon #4)**. That's when the seller reduces the price as an incentive for you to buy it. *Discount* is a term I'm pretty sure you know, but I am covering the basics, so I thought it was worth tossing it in and making it Jargon #4.

With the deposit of your $2,000 and the discount of $500, the car is going to cost you $15,000. You explain to the sales guy that you can't afford the whole car right now, so you want to take the front left wheel, and you'll come back for the rest over time. Just kidding! You didn't want the front left wheel—it's the bumper you want. No! Stop it, Aaminah. Back on track, please.

Okay. You explain to the sales guy you can't afford to pay for it all right now. "No problem," he says. "We have a way to lend you the money. You can borrow $15,000 from us. We'll charge you $150 each month to do that. That number won't change. Each month, regular as clockwork, you'll pay $150 extra for borrowing the $15,000. We'll keep it really simple so you know exactly how much extra to pay us each month."

Like your no-longer-friend who wanted that extra $5, this guy is charging you $150 per month in interest. It's a special type of interest called **simple interest (Jargon #5)**. And it is really simple—you borrow the principal, and the cost to you for doing so is a fixed amount based on how much you borrowed. At the end of one year, let's say you've paid nothing back at all. You'd still owe $15,000 (the principal). You'd also owe $150 for January, $150 for February, and so on. At the end of the year, the simple interest you owed would be 12 times $150, or $1,800. Simple! You're nailing this. That's Jargon #5.

Different scenario now, but let's stick with the idea of simple interest. You have $10,000, and you want to deposit it in a bank. You find a bank that will give you $1,200 at the end of one year, just for keeping the $10,000 in the bank. To phrase it differently, they will give you $100 each month for lending them your $10,000. At the end of January, you'll have $10,100; at the end of February, you'll have $10,200, and so on through the end of the year. They are paying you simple interest on your deposit with them.

You are happy with that arrangement, so you deposit your $10,000 in the bank and go get a coffee from your favorite coffee shop to celebrate. As you are sitting there staring out the window, sipping your brew, and people-watching, something occurs to you. *Hang on! If in January the bank gives me $100 for my $10,000, which is 1%, then at the end of January I'll have $10,100. Now that I have an extra $100 in my account, surely for February they should give me $100 in interest for the original $10,000, but they should also give me $1 for the other $100 that is now sitting in my account. That means that at the end of February, I would have the original $10,000, plus $100 in interest for January, plus $100 in interest for February, AND I should have $1 in interest for January's $100 interest that I'd already earned. I think my interest should earn interest.* You're pleased with yourself, and the coffee is also really good. Unwittingly, you've just figured out **compound interest (Jargon #6)**. Boom shaka for Jargon #6! Compound interest—when interest you've earned from your principal begins to earn interest on itself.

Let's go back to that car you're paying off. Eventually you won't owe any money on it. Years later the car is yours, with no debt. Honestly, you should celebrate. That's massive. Out you go for a night of partying with your homies—not $5 interest guy; he's gone. No one liked him anyway. A few drinks into the night, you have an epiphany: *I'll sell the car and get a new one. It cost me $17,000, and I can put the $17,000 I make from selling it toward a new car.* The next day, you phone the car dealer and say you want to sell them back the car. *No problem,* they say. *We can offer you $11,000.*

"ELEVEN?" you shout into the phone. "I paid SEVENTEEN for it."

There's a confused silence at the other end of the phone. "Yes," the salesperson replies, "but you've been using it for several years, so it's older and has more miles on the odometer. Haven't you heard of depreciation?" If you hadn't heard of it before, you have now! **Depreciation (Jargon #7).** As you use things, they wear out, and their lifespan decreases, which lowers their value.

Your car has value, but not as much as when you bought it. If you really want to know what it's worth now, you can reduce the original purchase price by the amount of depreciation. This reduction is called netting—not the netting you get when you take lots of holes and tie them together with string. You know, to make a net...Oh, Aaminah, what a rib-tickler you are!

This netting gives you the net asset value. Yikes! That's more terminology for you. **Net asset value (Jargon #8)**—the real value of an item after you reduce the purchase price by the value it's lost from your use of it.

You decide to keep the car after all. But now you're curious. If it lost that much value because you had it a while and used it, what about the other things you own? How much have they lost, and how much are they worth now? Out comes your notebook or whatever you use to make lists, and on it you record **everything** you can think of that you own. You assume the $47.52 in your bank account is still worth the full amount—about enough to buy food for a few days or booze for a night. I know which one I'd choose. You complete your list with all the items you own, what you paid for them, and an estimate of what they might be worth now. The list is pleasantly long with some large numbers in the estimate column. *I wonder what they're all worth together*, you ponder. Whipping out a calculator, you add them all up. It's a healthy number, and you can bask in the glow of financial progress.

Damn! Just as you were thinking about how well you were doing, you realize you forgot about the $100 you still owe Green Weed Jimmy. You probably need to take that off the total because once you pay him, you won't have that money anymore. Oh yeah, and the $240 overdraft at the bank—you still need to pay that. The more you think about it, the more you remember there's quite a lot you owe people. Hmmm. That healthy number is going down pretty quickly. So you make a list of everything you owe—your list of liabilities. Yes, that's another termin-o-thingamabob. *Nice*, you think.

With a sigh, you add up your list of liabilities and subtract that amount from the total value of what you own—what you're worth. The number you get is called your **net worth (Jargon #9)**. I feel that's worth a tennis expression—ace!

How do you feel about that—your net worth? Are you doing well? Is there room for improvement? Are you on target to be a millionaire by 25...or ever?

Pause for Thought

Take a moment here and step back. Think of all the concepts in just that one paragraph about net worth. You had to know about any down payments you've made, the principal you've borrowed, any interest you've paid on the principal, and any depreciation over the life of an item so you know what it's worth now. That's incredible when you think about it. Well done. Are you feeling empowered?

There's one last term to learn. You get money from a variety of sources, right? Add them all together. Yes, include even the money your roommate paid you to not post pictures of last night's events (what happens in Vegas...and all that). Now think of who you give money to—the grocery store, the owner of the home you're renting, the utility companies, and Jimmy down the hall who you slip 10 bucks to occasionally in return for a little bag of green weed. Yes, you do have to include that cash to Jimmy. Sorry, but this is your personal finances, and it's often these little "luxuries" on the side that take the biggest bites out of your money. Are you back with me? Cool. That list you have of the money that comes in—roommate bribes, other incomes on the side—add them together. Now add up what you pay for Jimmy's green bags and everything else. Add those expenses together. Now the last step. Subtract all the expenses from all your income. The insignificant number you're left with is your cash flow figure.

Wow! You. Are. Good. At. This. **Cash flow (Jargon #10)** —the difference between your income and your expenses.

Because you've done so well, you now have two choices for how to continue with this book. You can move on to the next chapter, or you can look at some actual figures. If I were you, I'd hang around a bit longer. Seeing examples in black and white can really help you learn.

1. Principal can mean one of two things, depending on which way the money is flowing.

- When borrowing, it is the original sum of money you borrowed from a bank or lender. This could be in the form of a loan, overdraft, or other form of debt. For example, if you borrow $10,000 from your bank for a home renovation, the principal balance is $10,000. As time passes and you make loan payments, the principal balance reduces until the debt is cleared.
- When saving or investing, it is the original amount of money you put into a savings account or other investment. For example, if you put $500 into your savings account, $500 is your principal balance.

The importance of the principal amount is that it is used to calculate interest.

2. Interest

- When borrowing, interest is the amount you pay for the privilege of borrowing money from someone. It is the amount they need as compensation for loaning you the money.
- When saving or investing, interest is the money you earn as compensation for putting your money into a bank or other financial institution. The money you deposit is thought of by the bank as a loan from you to them, so it is their cost of borrowing money from you.

3. Simple vs. Compound Interest (warning: a few easy formulas ahead)

i) Simple interest

Interest calculated on the principal amount only

How much interest would you earn if you invested $2,000 at a simple annual interest rate of 8% per year?

P denotes the principal, which equals $2,000 (P = $2,000).

R denotes the simple interest rate, which is 8% (R = 0.08, which is 8% expressed as a decimal).

T denotes the length of time in years that the money is invested.

B is the balance at the end of the year.

I is how much interest is earned, and for a single year it's calculated as follows:

I = P x R x T

I = $2,000 x 0.08 x 1

I = $160

Each and every year, you will earn $160 in simple interest. In order to know the balance at the end of 20 years, use the following formula:

B = P + (P x R x T) where (P x R x T) is the formula we used above for calculating only the interest part.

B = $2,000 + ($2,000 x 0.08 x 20)

B = $2,000 + $3,200

B = $5,200

ii) Compound interest

Interest calculated on the principal amount as well as on any interest earned to date. The formal name for interest that has been earned is accrued interest.

Year	Balance at Year Start	Interest Earned in Year	Balance at Year End
Year 1	$2,000	$2,000 x 0.08 = $160	$2,160.00
Year 2	$2,160	$2,160 x 0.08 = $172.80	$2,332.80
Year 3	$2,332.80	$2,332.80 x 0.08 = $186.62	$2,519.42
And so on...			

The formula changes a little because the interest rate has to reflect that it pays interest on interest. This is done as follows:

$$B = P (1 + R)^t$$

After 1 year

$B = \$2,000 (1 + 0.08)^1$

$= \$2,000 \times 1.08 = \underline{\$2,160}$. That's the same number as the table above.

After 2 years

$B = \$2,000 (1 + 0.08)^2$

$B = \$2,000 \times 1.08^2$

$B = \$2,000 \times 1.1664$

$B = \underline{\$2,332.80}$. Again, that's the same number as the table above.

After 20 years

$B = \$2000 (1 + 0.08)^{20}$

$B = \underline{\$9,321.91}$

Compound interest earns $4,000 more than simple interest over the same time frame. This is known as the power of compounding, and we will discuss it throughout this book.

4. Assets are anything you own that has financial value. That includes cash, funds in the bank, retirement account balances, stocks/bonds/mutual funds, real estate, vehicles, and so on.

5. Depreciation is the lowering of an asset's value by using the asset.

6. Net assets are the things you own with financial value after that value has been reduced by depreciation.

7. Liabilities are what you owe (e.g., bills, amounts owed on cars and houses, credit card balances, loans, etc.). It doesn't have to be owed to a company; you could also owe it to family and friends.

8. Net worth is the sum of all assets minus the sum of all liabilities (i.e., the difference between what you own and what you owe).

9. Income is money that flows to you either from work done or investments made.

10. An expense is any money that flows away from you due to costs incurred.

11. Cash flow is the sum of all income minus the sum of all expenses for a period of time.

There are a lot of people out there today who have high net worth but are still living paycheck to paycheck because cash flow is low. This is normally because the main asset in net worth calculations is the home they live in. So if you've got a nice 6- or 7-figure house, your net worth might be very high.

However, if you haven't got anything left at the end of the month after paying the mortgage and other expenses on that home, your cash flow is close to nothing. If you were to retire tomorrow, how would you sustain that lifestyle without the income from your job?

Two key takeaways from this chapter:

1. Do not underestimate the power of compounding.
2. Always keep a close eye on your cash flow. It is a much more accurate indicator of your financial situation.

ACTION PLAN – DAY 1

- Learn the jargon as best you can.
- Highlight the key definitions or simply bookmark this page so you can refer back to this later, if needed.

THE 9 GOLDEN RULES OF PERSONAL FINANCE

Money can't buy you happiness, they say. I'd say my designer Louboutin heels make me pretty happy, but never mind. I'm sure we can all agree that money *can* help buy you freedom. It can help you achieve your most ambitious goals and dreams, whatever they may be. And money gives both you and those you love security in life. Pause for a minute and think about that before you decide to give up and put this book away on a dusty shelf, never to be seen again.

These 9 Golden Rules are the principles upon which you should base all future financial decisions. However, if you need a real-life example to emulate, look no further than my old friend Warren Buffet (I'm kidding; he has no idea who I am). Buffett is easily the most recognizable investor in the world and worth tens of billions of dollars. He tells the story of picking up a penny on an elevator floor and then turning to the shocked execs with him and saying, "That's the start of the next billion." Unlike most of us, he understands money and how easily large results from small. Just like the rest of us, he's also made some bad decisions and investment choices over the course of his career. He has, however, also turned $107,000 in 1956 into a company where each share was worth more than $100,000 in 2006. Dubbed the "Oracle of Omaha," Buffett is famously frugal, eating a cheap McDonald's breakfast every day and living in the same home he bought in 1958. He knows money inside and out and is a prime example of someone who lives and breathes the golden rules of personal finance.

RULE #1 – MONEY NEEDS ORGANIZING

Houses, wardrobes, desks, cupboards—they all need to be organized so we can find the things we need when we need them. Clothes need to be washed and laundered. Likewise, money needs organizing and laundering.

Ah—maybe don't launder your money. It tends to get stuck on the inside of the washing machine. Coins particularly don't do well. And for some strange reason, the IRS tends to take an interest in your washing machine at that point, so let's leave that step alone for now.

Then how do we keep our money organized? We use something magical called a budget. *What the heck is a budget?* you say. Well, clearly it has something to do with organizing our money, and it's no more, really, than writing down what you are going to spend your money on and then seeing if you can stick to that. Seriously, it's no more challenging than that. I use a spreadsheet (Microsoft Excel), but there are plenty of mobile app options, too. It's too easy for your financial life to get messy, for bills to be left unpaid, and for crippling debt to accumulate if you don't organize your money. You need to consistently track what's going in and out of your accounts and keep all the information in one place. The thought of organizing your money might sound intimidating, but I'm going to walk you through each step in Part 2 of the book. Don't worry; I'm a top teacher, so it'll be easy street.

RULE #2: MONEY NEEDS CONTROLLING

Kids, eh. Little terrors. We do love them, though. Those critters never do a thing you ask them. *Sorry, Mom, I got distracted. Sorry, Dad, I got lost in my game.* So you pick up that wet towel on the floor (again), put the dirty dishes in the dishwasher (again), and do all the other small jobs they should have done but didn't. The good news is that they do eventually grow up and somehow find out how to do all these jobs themselves, normally when their choices are limited to either eating off the floor, or actually washing that aging dirty plate.

Money is like a kid but less cuddly and, thankfully, much more responsive to instruction. If you wave your credit card at a payment terminal and shout "Avada Kedavra" in your best

Harry Potter impersonation, the clerk will die an instantaneous death in a flash of green light accompanied by a rushing noise, and you can walk away without paying for the item. On the other hand, in the unlikely event that the clerk doesn't die, money from your credit card shoots through the ether and lands in the store's bank account. The money doesn't complain; it doesn't say *No, I won't*, folding its arms and sitting with a grumpy face on the edge of its bed. Instead, it meekly jumps from your account to theirs and sits with a smile, panting like a Labrador that's just retrieved a ball. At that point, you can say, "Good money!" but clerks do tend to look at you a little funny if you do.

Like that Labrador, money is **loyal**. It will work for you without complaining. But it needs guidance from you. Every dollar you earn needs to be assigned a task and a place to go. If you do this, you will always be in control. You will always know what you can and can't spend. And you're much less likely to buy that Rolex or Gucci handbag just because you feel sad and need some retail therapy.

You can either work for money or make your money work for you. I know which one I prefer. If you're sitting around worrying about how you'll pay your bills because you don't know what money you have available to spend, then your money isn't working for you. For instance, you decide to spend $200 on a super expensive meal with your significant other because you looked at your bank balance and saw $2,000 sitting there. "Damn girl, I'm rich," you tell yourself. And boy, do you enjoy that meal. A few days go by, and you realize in a panic that you still need to pay some bills that month. Man, are you regretting that meal!

That's what the budget you'll be making later on in this book is for. With a great budget, you would have seen the $2,000 sitting there, looked at your list of upcoming expenses, and accepted that most of that money would be used for rent, bills, and groceries. There would have been only $20 for fun stuff like eating out and entertainment. So you would have gone out for burgers and fries at your favorite fast-food restaurant instead. You would have still eaten out, but you would have restrained yourself and saved enough to pay those pesky bills on time. Maybe you can allocate more money to fun someday. For now, you're stuck with a low-key burger.

In addition to simply tracking your income and expenses, a budget (if done correctly) serves as a constant reminder of your financial goals. You will set spending goals, assigning X amount to rent, food, vacations, and so on. You'll know where to look when you have to make a financial decision. That applies to a decision as small as what to eat tomorrow and as big as buying a house. Rule 2 takes care of you and saves you from making any silly decisions in the moment.

RULE #3 – PRIORITIZE AND SPEND "CONSCIOUSLY"

Have you heard of Ramit Sethi? I hadn't either. He is another personal finance expert who introduced the idea of conscious spending in his book *I Will Teach You to Be Rich*. It's a simple idea about spending money more on what you enjoy and less on what you don't (Sethi, 2019). This gives you the most personal satisfaction for every dollar spent.

I'm a shoe girl. Love them. Don't call me Imelda, though. I've only bankrupted my husband—not a whole country—for my shoe collection. LOL. Don't worry, he's not bankrupt. Yet. Winking emoji.

Since I enjoy buying shoes more than eating out, according to Sethi, I should prioritize my shoe buying and deprioritize eating out. That seems sensible as long as I keep my shoe spending within the applicable category of my budget, which I keep telling myself is not food or any of the other essential categories, no matter how hard that gets. My solution is to cook at home, which is cheaper than eating out and leaves me with more money to spend on shoes. That brings us to a key point. Are you spending your money on the right things? It's all well and good for me to say I like spending money on shoes, but if my utilities aren't paid because I've splurged on some Jimmy Choos, then I'm not managing my money.

The important point is that your outgoings need to be prioritized. Think of a sinking ship and the captain calling out, "Women and children first! Men last. Camels after the men." In money terms, that's you, the Captain of Your Money Ship, shouting, "Food and shelter first! Jimmy Choos last!" And you probably won't be buying a camel, so you can ignore that.

In summary, some expenses are absolutely necessary, some you can take or leave, and some are simply frivolous if we're honest with ourselves. The absolutely necessary category includes your rent or mortgage, utilities, and groceries. These things keep you alive. Nearly as important but not quite are expenses such as insurance premiums, vehicle expenses, and debt payments. Note: no shoes in either of those priority categories. You might not enjoy spending money on these priority items, but they're essential. Minimize them to realistic levels, or work to make sure they don't increase more than they need to. That will leave you with more money to allocate toward the things you do enjoy (note: like shoes).

RULE #4 – LET YOUR MONEY GROW OLD

I'm going to be serious for a brief moment. I'll try not to do it too often.

I am not exaggerating when I say that this principle will change your life. Aging your money refers to spending money that is at least 30 days old. That means when your income comes in, don't touch it as much as possible. In time, you'll have saved at least one month's living expenses and can pay your bills from the saved amount.

Why is this so powerful? Delaying spending gives a greater appreciation for the money you have. That greater appreciation in turn helps you delay spending. It becomes easier and easier to say no to frivolous purchases, and the more you say no, the greater your net worth becomes. You also build good spending habits that become ever more crucial as your income rises.

Phew. That's enough seriousness.

RULE #5 – LIFE HAPPENS. ROLL WITH IT

In the movie *Forrest Gump*, Tom Hanks said, "Life is like a box of chocolates. You never know what you're gonna get" (Zemeckis, 1994). You could get some delicious, rich, nutty chocolate, or you could pick out the sticky one with a strange strawberry filling. Hanks was right. We never quite know what's going to happen next in life. When things don't go according to plan, you could run head first into a wall and knock yourself out. I don't advise it, though, since that would damage the wall, which might cost you quite a bit. So be kinder to *yourself* the wall.

We've talked about budgeting—keeping your finances tidy and telling your money where it needs to go. That's all good, but know that there will be hiccups along the way. There will always be unexpected expenses. The best way to deal with that is to have safeguards in place to protect yourself and your family. Get insurance—life, health, disability—so if anything goes seriously wrong, you're covered. Have an emergency fund in place (that's something I hammer on over and over like a broken record). That means saving up at least six months' worth of living expenses to cover you in case you lose your job or your business. Having a budget will help. But having the right mindset is also critical. Don't get caught up when "life happens". The most successful people are those who hit a wall, get some bruises, but pick themselves right up and carry on (while simultaneously icing those bruises).

Take some advice from the song *Roll with It* by the English rock band Oasis:

> *"You gotta roll with it*
> *You gotta take your time*
> *You gotta pay what you pay*
> *Don't let unexpected expenses that crop up out of*
> *nowhere get in your way"*

I might have misremembered those words. Oops.

The absolutely fantastic thing about having a budget is that it lets you know what the tolerance is for "life happening." Life is unpredictable. You may have planned, for instance, to put $200 in savings next month. Then your sink springs a leak, so now you know you can afford $150 for the unexpected plumber expense. Or an old flame comes into town for the weekend, gets in touch, and you go out for an unexpected party. You've got the money, so why not? At the party, your old friend confesses they still love you. You start crying and say, "I love you, too." Before you know it, you're married and have three kids—all because you had an extra $200 to spend. At that point, you'd better have a budget, coz kids are a money pit. A deep one.

RULE #6 – UNDERSTAND DEBT, AND USE IT WISELY

I'm not going to tell you to never get a credit card or a loan and to use cash for everything. That would be (1) nearly impossible to achieve and (2) just plain wrong. Not all debt is bad, and in fact, it is necessary. You just need to understand the different types, how to use them to your benefit, and how to avoid drowning in debt. In Chapter 6, we will discuss debt in detail and go through some case studies, too. Enjoy!

RULE #7 – PREPARE FOR THE FUTURE

Yes, you're probably just a teenager or in your early 20s. And yes, you've got important things to worry about such as what to wear at next week's party. But do you remember cramming for your exams the night before on zero hours sleep and 50 cups of coffee? Do you also remember spending the night wishing you had started earlier? But it was too late by then. At the risk of sounding overly philosophical, life is like an exam, only you can't cram the night before. You have to start now.

Start saving for retirement, a house, and even *your* kids' college funds. It all has to start now. Putting money aside for things that are seemingly centuries away is a tough thing to do. But it's also the smartest thing to do. In later chapters, we will talk about the best way to do this, how to prioritize what to save for and when, and the best ways to beef up your retirement fund so you can spend those golden years touring South America on a yacht or private jet. That's my plan, anyway. I should probably tell my husband.

RULE #8 – DIVERSIFY YOUR INCOME STREAMS

How do you get to college or work? Do you drive, take the bus, ride your bike, or get on a train? I'm guessing you have a preference, but the point is that most, if not all, of those options are available to you. If your car breaks down, you can ride your bike (although it may take a few hours longer). If it's raining, you can catch the bus instead. You have diversified your transportation options. In a similar manner, I encourage you to diversify your income streams.

Relying on one source of income is not only risky, it's also very limiting. You could lose your job at any time, or personal circumstances may not allow you to work that job in the future. A robot could replace you. Who knows what could happen? That's why you need multiple, varied income streams. That also allows you to make more money. The more you have coming in, the more you can do with your life. It's as simple as that.

We talk about income streams in Chapter 10—how many to have, how to decide which ones to focus on, and how to scale those income streams so you're not working 100 hours a week for the rest of your life.

RULE #9 – INVEST FOR THE LONG TERM

You know what compounding means now. And you know how powerful it is. The problem is that it requires patience. The best way to build patience—have children. They never do anything you want when you want them to. Take my parents, for instance. They were hoping I'd grow up years ago. Investing to make money for the short term is the biggest mistake new and inexperienced investors make.

Why do we incorrectly tend to invest for the short term? Because long-term investing is boring and takes patience. Short-term investing is exciting; there's a thrill to it, sort of like gambling. It's because making big bucks 10 years down the road usually means dealing with some short-term losses, and that can be painful. But it's also because we're always in a hurry for everything. We youngsters, today's youth, us Millennials, always want everything quickly, fast. It's why we pay for Amazon Prime because 48 hours for deliveries is "*so* yesterday, honey!" Even 24 hours is suuuch a wait. Then we get our delivery, pop the item in the cupboard, and don't look at it for months. It's why I have Alexa set up in my room to turn on the lights for me or tell me what the weather is. I want answers fast. With investing, you can't think like that. It is not a get-rich-quick scam; it's a get-*really*-rich-slowly-and-for-a-much-longer-time approach.

Let your money compound over time (a phrase you'll hear me parrot throughout this book). I talk about it in Chapter 11, but having the right investing mindset is key. Prioritize the long term over the short term, and you will reap the rewards.

ACTION PLAN – DAY 2

- Reflect on the above principles and decide which of them, if any, you are already implementing in your life.
- Think through what is important to you—why are you reading this book and embarking on this personal finance journey? What's your end goal? Is it to be debt-free? To save up for a house? Or do you just want to be financially free? What does financial freedom mean to you?
- This next exercise is larger than we can possibly cover here, but if you haven't done it already, take some time

to pull together a vision of where you want to be in a few months or a few years. Some people do this by using vision boards. A vision board is basically a huge colorful poster full of images and quotes that reflect the financial goals you want to achieve. These goals should align with your life goals and ambitions.

- For more information on money vision boards, tips, and ideas on how to make one, take a look at this link: https://selfmadeladies.com/vision-board-that-works/. It doesn't matter *how* you do it as long as you do it.

II

THE NITTY GRITTY OF $ MANAGEMENT

3

OH MONEY, WHERE ART THOU? – HOW TO CONDUCT A PERSONAL SPENDING ANALYSIS

I n the previous chapter, we looked at why tracking income and expenses is important. For me, it's mostly because I want to buy shoes and go on vacation and be able to afford the plumber. Now we're going to look at where our money actually goes—behind the sofa, under the bed, in the street? I'm going to take you through a step-by-step process for reviewing your past income and expenses. If you don't have a clearer picture of your finances by the end of this chapter, try cleaning your glasses.

GETTING STARTED

Looking at your past finances can be uncomfortable the first few times you tackle it. The point is to give you a sense of what you've spent money on already, and this will give you the framework to plan how you might be spending money in the near future. To help you get to that point, it's time to take some action. Grab a flat piece of wood with no splinters that's big enough to sit on. Take some long nails and hammer them through the wood until you have a bunch of nails sticking out the other side. Then put the piece of wood on a chair with the nails sticking up and sit on it. That's what I call *uncomfortable.* Budgeting will be a breeze after that.

I'm kidding, you know. Don't hammer long nails through wood and then sit on it. Short nails work fine.

Cool. So where are we? We need something to make notes on or in.

Now that you're sitting (un)comfortably and before you begin the comparatively less painful task of looking at past spending, you need to choose a method for recording the work you're about to do. If none of the following software options resonate with you, don't forget trusty ol' pen and paper. It's worked for thousands of years—well, the pen didn't; that ran out and needed replacing. And the dog ate the notebook. Okay, so there are limitations with Ol' Trusty, but in the absence of anything else, it's better than a poke in the eye with a pencil by an angry accountant.

The classic tool is a spreadsheet (not spread sheet—that's making your bed and needs to be done slightly more often than budgeting). Google Sheets and Microsoft Excel are the stand-out candidates here. To help you review your past spending and create a budget, I've created an awesome toolkit you can use. Download it at www.30daymoneyschool.com.

As a starting point, I always recommend using a spreadsheet since it's not as labor-intensive as pen and paper but gets you to focus on and understand the process more so than an app.

Not everyone likes the classics, though. If you're a modern creature, an on-the-go guy or gal, then at the end of Chapter 4 is a list of apps for both Android phones and the other one. They're mostly for budgeting, which is why I haven't listed them here, but some are also good for reporting back to you what you've spent money on and flagging when you're overspending in certain areas. Remember later on that spreadsheets are a great option for budgeting. For now, we'll use them just to review past spending.

Now we have what we need to make notes *on*. Next we need something to make notes *about*, so it's time to gather together whatever you can that's got some numbers on it. Menus, telephone books, and brochures are good, but even better are your receipts and financial statements. Most of our spending these days is by credit or debit card, so our financial institutions will have a record of the gushing of hard-earned e-Benjamins we handed over and who we handed them over to. They'll also let us know about the dribbles of e-Hamiltons into our accounts that we sometimes call income. I know a few people who still receive their statements on thinly-sliced trees, but most people nowadays have access to online statements they can download so they don't have to write it all out tediously. Don't forget to download from other payment providers such as PayPal or your favorite cryptocurrency wallet.

That's a great start.

If you're totally exhausted at this point, you're more than entitled to take a break. You've earned it. Grab that Kit Kat, a cup of coffee (the one you didn't have because you were investing in your future), add a splash of whisky, and settle down for a binge video session. What are you watching at the moment? I couldn't find any great series on bookkeepers or accountants with dramatic music in the background as they did or didn't reconcile their monthly accounts, so I've been re-watching *Game of Thrones* instead. I guess Ben Affleck does a reasonable job of a corporate accounting reconciliation in *The Accountant*. Give that a watch instead if you are one of the rare breeds who don't think *GOT* is the best show known to man. And if you've never heard of it, I just don't know what to say.

Alrighty then. Break's over. For the sake of brevity, I'm going to assume you are tapped into the magical ether of online accounts rather than a paper equivalent. Saves time. Mine and yours. Because I don't like waffling on about irrelevant things that mean nothing and simply cause us to lose our train of thought. Okay, now where was I?

Have you downloaded your bank statement yet? Think of it like a newspaper. Each line is a headline but without a story. That story is actually kept on the receipts you've collected. That's right, collected. Yes, you do need to collect them. If this is your first time creating a budget and you've *not* collected your receipts, that's okay. Rookie mistake, easily done. I keep asking my husband where mine are. If you haven't collected them, start now for the next time we sit on our seat of nails together.

Do you use cash much? Some people do. I try not to as it's often harder to track. I withdrew $50 three days ago, but I've only got $2.21 in my wallet. What on earth did I spend $48 on? Now, huge bonus marks if you immediately thought, *That's not $48; it's $47.79*. You're virtually a pro already. Back on the cash spending. Without receipts, I'd draw a blank. Actually, I draw a blank on most things I did three days ago; money just happens to be one of them. From now on, really try to collect receipts. I know the Amazonian trees are crying at all the paper you're collecting, but you can recycle them when you're finished. And with all your extra money, you can make a donation to Save the Rainforests.

UNDERSTANDING CASH FLOW

By now you should have decided on a method to review your past spending and have hopefully gotten hold of your bank statements and receipts. If you've decided that you want nothing to do with pen, paper, Excel, or Google Sheets, I still recommend reading on. While apps are great for automating processes, it is still crucial to understand the underlying concepts. This is similar to how schools teach you division and multiplication. First, learn how to do it with a pen, paper, and your brain. Then you can have a calculator. This section is about understanding how to classify the various income and expense types.

Income: All the Money Coming In

People tend to know more about how much money is coming into their account than how much is leaving it. And it's pretty simple; any cash flowing into your account is income. That includes blackmail money, theft, and drug sales, but also your salaries, tips, gifts, and anything else. Ever bought a pair of heels one size too small because the deal was that good, but your actual size was out of stock? Yeah, the refund for that also counts as income. In the example below I've listed a bunch of things that can be called income. Some of them will be applicable to you, and others will not. I don't make any money from drug sales, for instance. You might, but I don't. That's because I give them away.

Month of: September	
Type of Income	**Amount Earned per Month ($)**
Pay slips	$3,000.00
Tips	N/A
Bonus	$500.00
Commission	N/A
Interest Income	$50.00
Side Hustle	$200.00
Dividends	$100.00
Gifts	$50.00
Refunds	$20.00 (*I knew* they wouldn't fit...)
Benefits	N/A
Financial Support	N/A
Other	N/A
Total Income ($)	**$3,920.00**

Remember, income can vary from month to month. When we come to the budgeting work in the next chapter, it's always best to assume the lowest value for income. This is called being conservative. For now, there's no need to write anything down. Just think about which categories work for you, and feel free to create your own. If you would like a copy of the above table, go to www.30daymoneyschool.com.

Expenses: All the Money Going Out

Understandably, we're going to focus largely on the money that's leaving your account. First, let's look at the different types of expenses you can incur.

Payments by Time Frame

Payments of the Same Amount Each Month

Some expenses each month tend to stay the same, such as rent or car payments. You could say they're a fixed amount. What could we call a payment that's fixed each month? A stable expense? That will confuse the horse riders. A set expense? Might spark an alert with the tennis gambling authorities about match fixing. Oooh...*fixing* is a good word—let's go with that. An expense that's fixed each month we'll call a fixed expense, which everyone else already calls it. Probably should have led with that.

Payments That Change Each Month

Then we've got some expenses that can vary each month. Expenses that vary—I think we'll just go ahead and call them variable expenses. Good, let's do that. What do you spend a bit more on one month and a bit less on another month? More booze in your birthday month and December? Some lingerie for your other half? No, not your top or bottom half—I mean as a present for your partner, your regular partner. Sneaky gifts for a piece on the side, while they do count toward your budget, are a bad idea, particularly if your regular partner helps you with your finances. They will spot your philandering. So to be clear, it's the piece on the side that's the bad idea. Anything spent on them is just compounding a bad decision. It might even come back to you with compound interest. Ha ha. That's just me making a funny little accountant joke.

Utilities vary each month. You might pay for heating in the winter or cooling in the summer, or both if you live in Toronto. Groceries, clothing, fuel, entertainment, eating out—these are all examples of variable expenses to keep track of. If you want a budget-busting idea, you can always make a lettuce shirt for your partner. That covers entertaining, clothing, and eating in, all in one simple step. Try to keep the budgeting figure realistic, but if you're not sure, assume a higher value, not a lower one. It's better to overestimate your expenditures and be welcomed by a few extra bucks at the end of the month than falling short.

Payments That Only Happen Once a Year

I'm sure you can remember how much the big-ticket items cost, things like rent, utilities, food, and cell phone charges. Those numbers are the ones you deal with every month, so they're easier to remember.

The tougher ones are those gorilla-sized expenses when you're on a chimpanzee-sized budget. They're big, and you don't see them very often, so we all have nightmares dealing with them. Take the ~~damn~~ wonderful holiday season for instance.

Remember Aunt Connie? Well, you haven't seen the old bat in 20 years but you're expected to buy her a gift. She's also bringing Cousin Lewis, her irritating, whiny son. I bet he's expecting something as well. He's bringing George, his best friend. And guess what? Yup, another present there. The alternative to buying them all presents is being banned from all future family gatherings.

Easy choice, then, since you don't like them anyway.

Just kidding. They are family after all, and if you look at your budget, you'll see there is some money there for presents, which you could use with some judicious planning.

Ah, the *planning* word again. What did we call that? Budgeting. Yup, you know it, you know it. Shimmy, Shimmy, Shake, Shake! But what if you haven't quite gotten to the point where you can look at the budget and see what money is left? Well, you could work it from the other direction. Think what you might need to spend, and then break that huge expense down into monthly chunks. Suppose you work out that you'll need to spend $2,000 buying gifts for friends and family in December. That's 12 times $167. Can you save $167 every month of the year? If you can't, then you have no business spending $2,000 on the holidays. Plead poverty—it works great and often means that presents *to you* are more generous.

There are other expenses that might happen once a year. Car insurance, taxes, an annual check-up for your loyal Labrador at the vet. If you're super-organized and on top of it, you can also budget for deductibles on all your insurance policies. Don't forget subscription services such as Amazon Prime and Netflix, as well as services such as cloud data backup.

Annual payments are simple in principle to deal with. Estimate the annual total and divide by 12, making sure you save that much money each month. If it looks like you can't afford to save that much, you need to cut your spending until all of these expenses fit in your budget. Here are a few handy tips: "forget" people's birthdays (saves on presents), go out for dinner with your parents (they can pay), save bus fare by running behind the bus, and save even more by running behind a taxi. Don't say this book isn't filled with amazing and useful handy hints. That's my job-*this book isn't filled with amazing and handy hints.* Oh well.

Payments That Happen Infrequently

Buying furniture or paying for the costs of moving can be really expensive, but they happen so infrequently that they're difficult to budget for. So we're not going to bother, *except* when you foresee them happening in the next 12 months.

The same is true of any planned vacations. Work out what that dream trip in the summer is going to cost you. That much, huh? In your dreams. That is why they call it a dream trip because you only get there if you're tripping.

Rainy day fund money—think of it as emergency funds and thank the heavens that you don't live in Mawsynram in northeastern India. It's the rainiest place in the world, and everyone there is broke. You'd be better off moving to the McMurdo Dry Valleys in Antarctica—no rainy-day money ever needed there. Of course, you'll die of exposure, but there won't be any emergencies to pay for.

What's the point of this money if you ever get some in your bank account? It gives you some freedom to take a few risks with your money. Not "gambling risky" but "shrewd investment risky". At the very least, it needs to have enough money to pay for your living expenses for six months. Got it? Six months, not six minutes. I know it's a pipe dream for some, but there you go tripping again on that pipe.

Payments by Category

There isn't a lot to add here that we haven't already covered. Go through your statements and pick out the nature of the spending, just like you did for your income at the start. Below are the categories I use, but feel free to make up your own. Just make sure you're very clear about which expenses go where since there can be overlap. For example, your student loans are a form of debt repayment, but they can also be seen as an education expense. I'd keep any form of debt firmly in the debt category, but costs for books or resources that aren't covered by your student loan can go under education. For a detailed breakdown of what I include under each category heading, please view the 'Forecast' or 'Actuals' tab in my toolkit.

Month of: September	
Type of Expense	**Amount Spent Per Month ($)**
Housing (e.g., rent/ mortgage, one-off moving costs/refurbishing)	$1,500.00
Utilities (e.g., gas, water, electricity)	$500.00
Everyday expenses (e.g. groceries and cosmetic supplies)	$200
Health/medical expenses	$20
Transportation (car payments/fuel/public transportation)	$500
Education	N/A
Childcare	N/A
Technology (cell phone, Internet/cable)	$30
Entertainment (including eating out)	$200
Pets	N/A
Gifts (including donations)	$200
Travel (planned vacations)	$500
Insurance	$100
Debt Repayment	$20
Savings (including emergency fund/ retirement)	$0
Total Expenses ($)	**$3,770.00**

We've seen in the prioritization section (Rule #3, Chapter 2) that we need to spend money on the most important things first. So you can categorize your expenses by priority at the same time. I tend to use essential, important, bit of fun, frivolous.

- **Essential** – things you absolutely can't do without (rent, bills, groceries)
- **Important** – things that are super important but not essential. You don't want to cut down on these unless you have no other choice. I'd say saving for retirement and some insurance payments fall into this category.
- **Fun** – any expenses relating to fun, whether it's eating out, gym payments, or vacations
- **Frivolous** – These expenses are the silly ones. They are fun, but they aren't things you really love and are probably a waste of money. Do you really need subscriptions to both Amazon Prime and Netflix?

Feel free to create your own prioritization categories according to your situation.

Now, Let's Calculate Cash Flow

If you refer back to my sample income and expense tables, you'll see that my total income for the month of September was $3,920, and my total expenses were $3,770.

Total Income ($3,920) – Total Expenses ($3,770) = $150

So… $150 left over at the end of the month. That's a bit embarrassing if you ask me. If you look at my expense categories individually, I haven't really thought about my savings just yet. My debt repayment figure is next to nothing since I'm just making minimum payments when I have to. The next few chapters after this one go into savings and debt repayment in detail. In this case, I only have $150 left over to play around with, which is currently sitting idly in my checking account. This figure should be much higher, and that $150 should be used to pay off some debt or placed in a high yield savings account to accumulate interest at the very least. The purpose of this exercise is to get a clear picture of where you stand with your money. For me, the picture isn't looking great.

So how did I go about conducting this analysis? My go-to option is always Excel. I do use apps, but I wouldn't use one for this sort of retrospective analysis. Again, this is entirely your preference. But I would recommend giving the following exercise a go and making a decision after that.

HOW TO CONDUCT A PERSONAL SPENDING ANALYSIS IN 11 STEPS

Step 1: You should have done this one already, but I ramble on a lot. So in case you missed the memo, you need to gather at least three months of bank statements and receipts for payments made in cash. Most banks and credit card companies allow you to download your statements within a specific date range from their website. I would suggest doing this one month at a time, particularly if this is your first time.

This will look different for every bank or financial institution. But generally, you'll get a screen similar to the one below. The button "Statement options" will allow you to download your statement in your chosen format.

Step 2: Export your transaction history for month 1 in Excel format. Simply save the file as an Excel Workbook. If you're not able to do this, find a way to copy the data into a blank Excel document and save it. If you pay for a lot of things in cash, this is going to take a bit longer. You'll need to manually enter the dates and transaction amounts from each receipt into your spreadsheet. If for some strange reason you also earn a lot of money in cash (don't worry, I won't expose you), you'll also need to make a note of this in your spreadsheet.

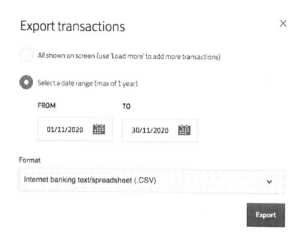

Step 3: Delete irrelevant columns such as those that list your account number, sort code, or overall balance after each transaction. You only really need four columns of data at this point: Transaction Date, Transaction Description, Debit Amount (money going out/expenses), and Credit Amount (money coming in/income).

To make your life easier, download my toolkit at www. 30daymoneyschool.com, and transfer your bank data there. All the following steps will be much easier to follow with my done-for-you template since the required columns, formulas, and tables are already in place for you.

Step 4: If you are using your own spreadsheet, add a column called "Expense Category" next to your expenses (money going out). Add another column called "Income Category" next to your income (money coming in). My template mentioned above already has these columns.

Step 5: Organize your income and expenses by category. The easiest way to do that is to sort the transaction description column from A to Z, in ascending order. That groups transactions of the same type together. For example, if you have made three payments to Uber Eats in the last month, you'll see that in one go. This makes it much easier to categorize each payment. On my Google Sheets toolkit or any Excel spreadsheet, you can simply highlight the whole table, click on Data, and then click on Sort range.

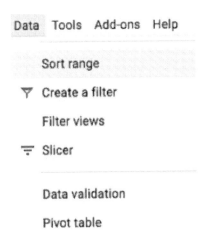

Now you need your data sorted according to "Transaction Description", so select that column. Check out Mr. Google or Mrs. YouTube if you aren't sure how or why to sort columns. It's a useful trick to have up your sleeve.

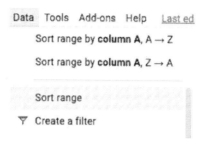

It is now much easier to categorize each transaction. Fill out the Category column for both money coming in and money going out. For a list of category types for both income and expenses, reference the tables I have included earlier in the chapter. For a full breakdown of what falls under each of these categories, view either the 'Forecast' or 'Actuals' Tabs.

Step 6: Now that all the transactions are categorized, you can sort your table by category. We're going to focus on expenses. So highlight the table, click on Data, and sort your range. Select the column where your expense categories are listed. See the example below.

Transaction Date	Transaction Description	Money Out (Expenses)	Category
9/13/2020	Amazon Prime	$12.99	Entertainment
9/14/2020	Audible	$14.95	Entertainment
9/18/2020	Netflix	$8.99	Entertainment
9/27/2020	Walmart	$50.00	Groceries
9/28/2020	Walmart	$150.00	Groceries
9/29/2020	Bank X Mortgage	$500.00	Housing

Now you can see everything you spend on for each category in a given month. We'll calculate totals and use those figures at a later stage. For now, you've got a much clearer idea of what your spending is like. There might even be some glaring expenses in the Entertainment category that you're feeling a bit guilty about right now...

Step 7: If you're using your own spreadsheet, add two more columns next to your expenses: Priority and Frequency. If you're using my toolkit, have a little stretch, do a little dance-you're over halfway through!

Step 8: Populate the Frequency column. For expenses that are monthly fixed expenses (e.g., mortgage payments), call these MF. For those that are monthly variable expenses, call them MV. Annual expenses can be labeled A, and one-off expenses can be O. In my toolkit, there's a key at the top to remind you of these labels. Of course, feel free to use your own.

Now, sort your data by Frequency so you can see your expenses grouped by frequency. When you start creating your budget in the next chapter, you'll be able to quickly refer back to this and see what your monthly and annual expenses are. For example, you can easily see across three months that your annual expenses are X, Y, and Z. Divide these amounts by 12, and throw them into your monthly budget plan. There may be others that come to mind, but this exercise certainly helps.

Similarly, for variable expenses, look for the highest value and assume that will be your average monthly expense when building your budget. That is the general rule of thumb and the safest way to do things. But use your common sense, too. Take groceries, for example. Let's say you spent $300 in month 1, $250 in month 2, and $600 in month 3. Sounds like *someone* had a party in month 3. Of course, that isn't what you need to budget for groceries for the next 12 months. Unless you're planning another party, I'd say $300 a month is a reasonable allocation for your groceries in this case. As for one-off expenses, they should only be accounted for if you are sure you'll be incurring that expense in the next 12 months.

Step 9: Populate the Priority column. This will help you understand whether your spending currently aligns with your goals. If your goal is to be financially free and retire in the next 10 years, you probably need the majority of your expenses to be essential and important, with a small amount of fun and absolutely no frivolity. As you know, my suggested prioritization categories are Essential, Important, Fun, and Frivolous. Feel free to choose your own.

Again, just click on data and sort your priority column in order to see your results grouped according to prioritization categories. If only two fall under essential and the remaining twenty rows are fun and frivolous, you know some serious changes are in order. This is another exercise that will be very useful and inform your budgeting work in the next chapter.

Transaction Date	Transaction Description	Money Out (Expenses)	Category	Priority
9/27/2020	Walmart	$50.00	Groceries	Essential
9/28/2020	Walmart	$150.00	Groceries	Essential
9/29/2020	Bank X Mortgage	$500.00	Housing	Essential
9/13/2020	Amazon Prime	$12.99	Entertainment	Frivolous
9/14/2020	Audible	$14.95	Entertainment	Fun
9/18/2020	Netflix	$8.99	Entertainment	Fun
9/30/2020	Gym	$25.00	Entertainment	Fun

Step 10: Repeat the above steps for the next two months. Ideally, you want a three-month view to inform your budgeting work in the next chapter. The more data you have, the better you'll understand your own financial situation and what steps to take to improve it.

Once you have done this, add a column called "Month" before your transaction date column and enter a fancy formula that lifts the exact date and pulls through the corresponding month. Again, either use my done-for-you template or ask Mr. Google for help. If you're already an Excel whiz, you'll know that the formula =TEXT(A2,"mmmm") returns a full **month** name such as January – December. Clever, huh?

Now, if you sort your data by "Transaction Date", everything will be organized nicely. It should look something like this:

Month	Transaction Date
Sep	9/13/2020
Sep	9/26/2020
Sep	9/27/2020
Oct	10/9/2020
Oct	10/20/2020
Oct	10/27/2020
Nov	11/8/2020
Nov	11/10/2020
Nov	11/20/2020

Be careful not to sort your data by Month otherwise Excel simply puts the Months in alphabetical order. And you get April's transactions appearing before February's.

Step 11: Once you have three months' worth of data in your spreadsheet, it's time for Pivot Tables. This is where the inner geek in me comes out. I *love* pivot tables.

These tables will provide you with a summary of your expenses according to category, priority, and frequency. All three angles are important in order for you to analyze your spending and understand where you may be going wrong.

If using my toolkit, all you need to do is head over to the "Personal Spending Summary" tab. Assuming you've completed all the previous steps, this tab will lift the data for you and auto-create the pivot tables. Magic! You should see something like this:

Total Expenses Split By:	Month			
Category	Sep	Oct	Nov	Grand Total
Entertainment	$119.00	$100.00	$120.00	$339.00
Groceries	$170.00	$200.00	$400.00	$770.00
Housing	$500.00	$500.00	$500.00	$1,500.00
Grand Total	$789.00	$800.00	$1,020.00	$2,609.00

Total Expenses Split By:	Month			
Priority	Sep	Oct	Nov	Grand Total
Essential	$670.00	$700.00	$900.00	$2,270.00
Frivolous	$119.00			$119.00
Fun		$100.00	$120.00	$220.00
Grand Total	$789.00	$800.00	$1,020.00	$2,609.00

Total Expenses Split By:	Month			
Frequency	Sep	Oct	Nov	Grand Total
A	$119.00			$119.00
MF	$500.00	$600.00	$620.00	$1,720.00
MV	$170.00	$200.00	$400.00	$770.00
Grand Total	$789.00	$800.00	$1,020.00	$2,609.00

Within seconds, Excel has given you a summary view of how much you spent per category across three months, how you prioritized your spending across three months, and also what your monthly and annual expenses looked like in each of those months.

I've also set it up to generate pivot tables for your income so you can see which revenue streams need to be beefed up. (Hint: It might be time to ask for a raise!)

Total Income Split By:	Month			
Category	Sep	Oct	Nov	Grand Total
Interest	$500.00	$500.00	$500.00	$1,500.00
Pay slips	$3,000.00	$3,000.00	$3,000.00	$9,000.00
Side Hustle	$200.00	$200.00	$200.00	$600.00
Grand Total	$3,700.00	$3,700.00	$3,700.00	$11,100.00

If you're using your own spreadsheet, please consult Mr. Google and Mrs. YouTube since they'll do a much better job of explaining how to create pivot tables from scratch.

Now it's pretty simple to work out your cash flow each month and your average cash flow across three months if you want to go the extra mile. Use Excel or pull out a calculator, and you've got a nice (hopefully 4- or 5-digit) figure to summarize your current financial situation. If it's not 4 or 5 digits yet, you'll get there. Don't worry.

As I promised, this book isn't about chucking information at you and sending you on your way. Here's your action list based on everything you've learned thus far.

ACTION PLAN – DAYS 3–6

- Figure out how to log in and access your bank statements online if that's something you haven't done before. Gather any receipts from the last three months.
- Check out www.30daymoneyschool.com for free access to the Excel template you can simply populate with your exported bank data. This also contains a key for all the suggested frequency and priority labels above. Feel free to change these as you see fit.
- If you prefer to use your own Excel spreadsheet, go you! Unless you're an Excel whiz, I'd suggest using

Google and YouTube to do some basic Excel training before attempting the task.

- Conduct your personal spending analysis in just 11 steps.
- Take a look at the whole picture of how you are spending your money (this would be your pivot tables). Compare this picture to the goals you wrote down in the previous chapter or that vision board that's on your wall.
- Identify any glaring problem areas. It could be a particular category you're overspending in or simply a prioritization issue. Does it look like most of your money is being spent on fun and frivolous things?
- Kick back and relax. You've done the hardest job already.

If you feel overwhelmed, this is natural. If you need reassurance, refer to this quote:

"You don't have to see the whole staircase, just take the first step."

— MARTIN LUTHER KING, JR.

4

YOUR GUILT-FREE SPENDING PLAN – CREATING AND MANAGING A BUDGET

Y ou've done the hard part in the previous chapter—really.

Budget.

Going through past statements is long and tedious.

Budget, budget, budget.

But it's so important because it tells you what you've already spent money on.

Budget, budget, budget, budget, budget.

Notice how if you say it long enough, it starts to sound like swearing.

Hit yourself on the finger with a hammer? Budget!

Trip over and land on your backside? In a puddle? Budget!

Run out of money before the end of the month? Budget!

That last one's not a swear word, by the way. If you really did run out of money before the end of the month, you really do need to budget.

Look, I get it. Lists are so boring. List this, list that, put numbers against them. Yawn. Where's my bed? The first time I even contemplated a budget was when I survived on Ramen noodles in college for two weeks. The first two weeks, I lived like a queen—out with my friends, partying and eating out. The second two weeks, I stayed home, miserable and adding empty noodle containers to the global pollution problem. I treated myself to an apple on Sunday. Hooray! The rest of the time it was Chicken Chow Mein noodles followed by Sweet and Sour Chicken noodles, followed by, well, by another type. I was so sick of noodles by the end of those two weeks that I swore I'd not go through that again.

"Don't tell me what you value. Show me your budget, and I'll tell you what you value."

— JOE BIDEN

Joe wasn't president when he said that, but Americans are realizing the value of a budget more and more with a recent study indicating that 8 in 10 Americans now use a budget. This is a 10% increase over the previous year ("Debt.com's 2020 Budgeting Survey," 2020). If you aren't one of those eight awesome people, that's okay. That's what I'm here for.

You see, my mama loaded my plate with vegetables when I was a kid. "It's good for you," she'd say. I bet your mom or dad was the same. I didn't really believe her then, and I probably don't really believe her now. But there is some literature that suggests the occasional veg might be worth something. Okay, okay. Lots of literature says having more than the occasional carrot actually is good for you. Stop waving that celery stick at me.

Budgeting is the "eat your veggies" of the personal finance world. I know it ain't sexy and you sure can't boast about it because who'd be the slightest bit interested, but financially speaking, if you do this well, you'll remain financially healthy. It's foundational to not eating Ramen noodles for half a month at a time.

That's what you have to keep in mind through all of this. A budget is your safety net. It's the seatbelt in your car—annoying to put on every time you get in—and my car beeps at me if I don't. Doubly annoying, but crucial in a car crash. It's the carbon monoxide detector in your home, the insurance policy you have on your home. It's all of these because it stops you from tripping up financially. Or if you are going to trip up, at least it's an early warning indicator.

At its core, it's a spending plan that normally lasts for the next 12 months. It identifies on a monthly or weekly basis all the income you're expecting and all your likely expenses and then shows you those times when you're spending more than you're earning. It identifies any gaps you have. As they say on the London Underground, "Mind the gap!" (that space between the platform and the door of the train). That's what you need to do —mind your financial gaps so you don't trip up.

If you want to get control of your money and future, you need a budget.

WHY HAVING A BUDGET IS THE KEY TO SUCCESS

If you're part of the 2 in 10 Americans who don't yet see the value of budgeting, I'm about to blow your mind. Here are some other amazing things that happen when you create and maintain a budget.

You'll Have a Bulletproof Plan to Turn Your Dreams into Reality

By bulletproof, I don't mean print out your budget, sticky-tape it to your chest, and go join a SWAT team. That would be dumb. You'd actually need at least two copies of your budget for that. Ha! Just kidding. It's more about making a solid base for the goals we all have for the future, whether it's buying a house, driving a fancy sports car, or having a full-blown Kim K level wedding. If you want to achieve those goals, you need to write them down and then put a plan in place to achieve them.

For anything that costs money, your budget is that plan.

Imagine this. You'd love to set out in your car and drive from New York to Chicago. The tank is full of gas, your vehicle is in top shape, and you're all set. You must be fine, right? You'll get there. There's just one problem. Where is "there"? You don't have a map, a navigation system, or even a route in mind. How can you possibly hope to reach your destination if you don't have a route in mind? Would you be crazy enough to try to *feel* or *estimate* your way toward Chicago? Perhaps a buddy could set off smoke signals from the Willis Tower to guide you. That might be a more realistic method than relying on your Jedi-like feel for the correct route.

Speak to people who don't maintain budgets, and they often say they have a feel for how much they're spending. They intuitively know where their money is going and don't need to track it. Sure, they'll probably be able to recite the big-ticket items such as rent, utilities, food, and cell phone charges. But I guarantee they have no clue where 10%–20% of their money goes. How much did they spend on Christmas presents last year? Do they have enough money to pay their annual car insurance? How large is their buffer if things go wrong?

If you don't know how to get to where you want to go, how can you hope to get there anytime soon? You're relying on luck, and luck is an unreliable partner.

You'll Only Spend the Money You Have

Spending is simple psychology, really. "I don't think, therefore I spend"—a misquote of René Descartes' famous saying, "I think, therefore I am." Putting a budget together means you'll know how much money is coming in, and that will help you think before you spend. Budgeting is like a speed limit on the road—except it's a spending limit. It tells you when you're spending too fast or getting close to the spending limit, which helps you slow down automatically. Does that mean it's a speedy spending limit or a spending speed limit? Who cares? I'm confused. You choose.

By spending the money you have as opposed to the money you don't, you'll end up valuing the things you have a lot more. This is a side effect of good financial management that you'll have to experience for yourself. I'm not going to spoil it for you by describing how great it feels. Actually, no, I am. It's amazing, particularly with the confidence it brings you.

You'll Save Money

Savings. Rainy-day money. Castle-in-the-storm money. Money in the bank creates a feeling of power. Trust me. Knowing you can knock a huge bill or just an unexpected bill out of the park is amazing. Savings are the Babe Ruth, the Serena Williams, the

Michael Jordan of personal finance—the one you go to when things get difficult.

That is because you've saved enough money to pay all your bills and have enough left over to pay for the unexpected expenses. Money in the bank is the best feeling in the world. It sets you free. There's no more going back to your parents, hat in hand, asking for handouts. For those who love independence, money in the bank will give it to you.

And budgeting is what puts the money there.

You'll Retire Happy

Damn, youngster! I know you're thinking, *Retirement? Are you kidding me? That's for old people.* You remember what we said, though, about the best time to plant a tree—it was 30 years ago. And do you know who's unhappy right now? Retirees—because they didn't plant their trees 30 years ago. Thirty years ago for a retiree is you, now. Don't buy into the belief that a strong government and economy will take care of you no matter what. Don't be the person working a steady job, assured by your employer that a fat pension waits for you on the other side of the retirement line, only to find that isn't true and it's too late to do anything about it.

Just think how many pension pots no longer exist because of bad management, or how many don't pay out as much as promised. What happens when employers ship jobs to India and China and outsource pension fund management to Wall Street? Those financial "experts" are the ones who invested this money into a bunch of financial WMDs and brought everything crashing down in 2008. Yes, those experts. Experts, schmexperts, my backside.

You can't bank on those payments being there. You need to actively work toward it.

Homes may not be worth as much as you'd hoped or, even worse, less than what you paid for them. Investments might be sitting at rock bottom. Inflation could be high, reducing what nest eggs you've stored for your chicks. You've got to plan for this. Plant one tree today. Remember, we're living longer than ever before, so we need the money to back up our longevity.

If you're living the high life on a high-life income, all's good. If the income becomes a low-life pension, that's gonna hurt. It's trite to reduce all of this to a lack of budgeting skills. But a lack of understanding of personal finance is to blame. It all begins with budgeting and goals. The right habits will let you avoid this sorry fate.

You'll be Ready for Emergencies

Life is unpredictable. As Murphy's Law states, "Anything that can go wrong will go wrong," except for Murphy's Law, which is always right. Go figure.

You can't fear the future. Don't be a pessimist, but be prepared. COVID-19 is a perfect example of things happening that are totally out of our control with its massive impact on incomes and job prospects.

A budget will help you prepare for these unexpected times.

You'll Conquer Your Weaknesses

Do members of Alcoholics Anonymous go to bars? Don't be silly. Or do gamblers go to the race track when they're trying to quit? Of course not! Going to the bar or the track is only going to lead to broken promises. You know already that I have a huge weakness for shoes. I even stashed them under my bed when I ran out of space in the closet. My budget helped me come to terms with my shoe-aholic tendencies; now I live on a shoe-string! I eventually sold my shoes on eBay for a whopping $2,000. More on that later.

If you want to see where you're frittering money, then the work you've done so far looking at past bank statements is going to help. If you want to avoid making the same mistakes in the future, you'll need a budget. Looking into the past helps identify your weaknesses, but to really conquer them, you need to plan in advance how to tackle them with a budget. Frittering on fritters isn't frittering, by the way, because we love donuts. Cut out all the other fritter-spend by looking it in the eye, staring it down with a Clint Eastwood glare, and taming those wild impulses to bring your spending back under control. You'll apply the brakes naturally, and you'll understand what you need to do to avoid going there again. So learn who you are through your budget.

You'll Get Back in Control

A budget is like a steering wheel—it helps you around corners. Take your hands off the wheel, and you'll crash. You'll crash even worse if you're speeding. A car can't make its own course, and your life shouldn't either.

The Doors say it best. "Keep your eyes on the road, your hands upon the wheel." Jim Morrison knew what he was talking about, and it wasn't about driving. He was really writing about budgeting and personal finance. And a roadhouse. And some honking. And letting a baby roll. Okay, who knows what he was talking about? It probably wasn't budgeting, in all honesty.

Maybe a better way to think of it is like an accountant's version of a *Final Destination* movie. In the film, they're driven to their death screaming in terror; in the accountant's version, a pen leaks in his pocket, and the ink goes on his shirt and the printout of his budget. Something like that.

You'd like to be in control of your destiny, wouldn't you?

You'll be More Flexible

If you overspend on one category, do what politicians do—take money from another worthy cause to cover the shortfall. Let's say you go $100 over budget on food, but there's still $70 left in your entertainment allowance and another $100 in your miscellaneous allowance. Share the love between the two, and take a bit from both until your $100 excess food spending is covered. They won't mind. Remember, money is loyal, and each dollar wants the best for you.

As long as your overall spending is under the limit, who cares what you're overspending on at the line item level?

It's true. Budgets work better than yoga. You'll be able to touch your toes in no time. Doh! Wrong flexibility. What I meant was you'll learn how to shift excess expenses from one category to another if you're overspending on other items. In short, you'll be a lot more financially flexible.

You'll Worry Less

A budget is to worry what Excedrin is to headaches. Both make the other disappear. I've stopped buying painkillers since I got my budget together. Now, let's move on and start putting all this into practice so you, too, can feel your worries withering away.

HOW TO BUDGET LIKE A PRO

The first and most important step is to decide on a budgeting method and plan out your allocations for each category. *What are allocations?* you say. Well, in order to enforce your desired spending habits, you need to sit down and work out how your income will be distributed across the various spending categories over the next 12 months. You can call this a spending plan or a forecast.

Remember all the incredible work you did in the previous chapter? Well, now it's time to use that. Here's what you need to do:

1. Evaluate your priorities. Are you happy with the way you have prioritized your spending over the last three months? What needs to change?

2. Calculate and note down your monthly expenses based on past spending. Remember, your fixed monthly expenses won't change, so that's easy. Work out a realistic average figure for your monthly variable expenses. And any annual expenses need to be divided by 12. Consider any one-off expenses, too, for the next 12 months.

Now that you have all this information, let's start building that forecast. There are many different ways to do this. Some personal finance experts recommend the 50-30-20 rule. In a nutshell, that means 50% of your income should be used to pay for your needs (essential spending), 30% ought to go toward your wants (non-essential spending), and the remaining 20% should be allocated to savings and debt repayment. I have to be honest, I don't agree with this. Here's my take: personal finance is personal. Such allocation formulas are good as a general starting point, but they are not helpful or useful on an individual basis. How much you spend on needs really depends on your situation. Are you still living with your parents at home, rent-free? Or are you paying for an apartment by yourself in a high-cost living area? That will drastically impact how much essential spending you have. Similarly, anyone who has high-interest debt has no business spending more money on wants than on debt repayment. It's like eating a salad to lose weight but having 10 ice cream cones for dessert. It violates basic common-sense principles. Others may have a lump sum to save up within a short amount of time (do I hear wedding bells?). My point is, *your* allocations need to match *your* goals.

Since we haven't covered savings and debt repayment in detail yet, it may be a bit difficult at this point to decide on your allocations for these two categories. And that's okay. The important thing is to get started, and you can adjust your goals as well as your allocations as you work your way through the book.

Create Your Spending Plan in 7 Simple Steps

The budget tracker I have created for myself (available for free at www.30daymoneyschool.com) adopts the zero-based budget system. A zero-based budget forces you to put each and every dollar you earn to work. It's a pretty rigorous method, but it works wonders. The idea is to allocate each and every cent of your income to something—expenses, savings, or just another pair of Jimmy Choos. At the end of the month, you should have no cash left over that is sitting idly. Don't think this means you have no money in your account. That's not the point. You can have money in your account, but that money should be serving a purpose—paying off debt, going toward retirement, or, you know, buying the latest Choos. You can implement this by using my spreadsheet or using an app. I've listed the best mobile apps at the end of the chapter.

Regardless of which software you use, it is crucial that you allocate X amount to each category and line item in your budget and don't exceed that amount each month. The total of all your allocations should equal your income. This ensures you are giving each and every dollar a job to do. You can download the actual budget planner for free at www.30daymoneyschool.com.

Step 1: Click on the "Forecast" tab. Forecast is just a fancy word for Spending Plan.

Step 2: Fill in your monthly income amounts. For each month, enter what you expect to earn alongside the correct line item (see screenshot below). If your income varies on a monthly basis, then assume the lowest value for the purposes of this exercise.

Forecast (12 months)	Jan	Feb	Mar	Apr
Total Income	$0.00	$0.00	$0.00	$0.00
Total Expense	$0.00	$0.00	$0.00	$0.00
Remaining Budget	$0.00	$0.00	$0.00	$0.00

Income					
Monthly recurring amount ($)	Monthly Income by category:	$0.00	$0.00	$0.00	$0.00
	Pay slip				
	Tips				
	Bonus				
	Commission				
	Other				

Step 3: Fill in your essential, fixed expenses for each month. If you enter a value in the column titled 'monthly recurring amount', it will auto-duplicate across 12 months, so you don't have to keep entering it manually. These are the expenses essential to your survival, which you have little to no control over. You don't have control over your rent or mortgage payments, for example. They are absolutely essential, and unless your landlord is your BFF (best friend forever), he ain't gonna cut your rent in half.

Forecast (12 months)		Jan	Feb	Mar	Apr
Total Income		$0.00	$0.00	$0.00	$0.00
Total Expense		$0.00	$0.00	$0.00	$0.00
Remaining Budget		$0.00	$0.00	$0.00	$0.00
Expenses					
Monthly recurring amount ($)	*Monthly Expense by category:*	$0.00	$0.00	$0.00	$0.00
	Activities				
	Allowance				
	Medical				
	Childcare				
	Clothing				
	School				
	Toys				
	Other				

Step 4: Decide up front how much you want to save and invest. Don't worry about this too much since it can be amended later. But you may already have some goals in mind. To become financially free as soon as possible, it's best to live on as little as possible. You don't need to be unkind toward yourself. It's just that you need to prioritize the long term ahead of the short term. Taking savings off the top and automating it so you don't have to decide "how much" every paycheck is the key

to saving successfully. If you only save "what's left", there will always be something shiny in front of you, begging to be bought.

Step 5: Fill in essential, variable expenses for each month. If you're running out of money at this point, find a way to adjust these expenses. Groceries, energy bills, and transportation costs are all examples of essential expenses that can be amended, if necessary. You don't need to drive a 2021 Chevrolet. Bills can always be negotiated, and there are many ways to cut down grocery spending. I'll be sharing some top-secret saving hacks later, so don't worry.

Step 6: Now that the essentials have been taken care of, you are free to spend the rest as you wish. Look at your overall percentages. Are you happy with how spending is being prioritized? Read the remaining chapters and adjust these as you go along.

As you fill out the sheet, your 'remaining budget' should keep reducing till you reach $0. The goal is to have this at $0, as that means that every dollar has been accounted for. See below:

Forecast (12 months)	Jan	Feb	Mar	Apr
Total Income	$1,000.00	$1,000.00	$1,000.00	$1,000.00
Total Expense	$1,000.00	$1,000.00	$1,000.00	$1,000.00
Remaining Budget	$0.00	$0.00	$0.00	$0.00

Step 7: Automate, automate, automate. It is so important that money for bills, debt repayment, and savings are leaving

your account automatically at the same time each month. You don't want to be doing this manually because you will forget. Trust me—*been there, done that.* The money left in your account should be just for discretionary spending.

You don't need to do this immediately, but I would highly recommend opening up four different accounts and setting up direct deposits from your paycheck to each of them. I'll go into more detail later on about the various types of savings accounts. So I'll keep it simple for now. ***Top tip:*** Ask your employer to arrange for your salary to be split up from the get go. This makes your life even easier. If they can't do this, it's relatively easy to set it up yourself. **Here are the four account types:**

1. Checking account for everyday spending (e.g., personal care, entertainment, miscellaneous expenses)
2. Checking account for paying bills and expenses (e.g., housing, debt, utilities, groceries)
3. Savings account for your emergency fund and short-term savings goals (e.g., birthdays, Christmas, new phone, new car)
4. Savings account for long-term savings goals (e.g., house, wedding, baby)

Once you have completed this exercise, all you need to do is start monitoring your activity on a monthly basis. The spread-sheet below breaks down each category into individual line items. You can edit these as you wish. The spreadsheet also helps identify problem areas. If you are not meeting your planned allocations for a particular category, the spreadsheet will highlight that. The Planned vs. Actual row will turn red if you are overspending.

Although apps are brilliant for this, I'd highly recommend starting off with a spreadsheet since it really makes you think about what you're doing and helps you understand the process. You can then move to apps at a later stage. But that decision is entirely yours.

Actuals (12 months)			Jan	Feb	Mar	Apr
	Income (Planned vs Actual)		$0.00	$0.00	$0.00	$0.00
	Expense (Planned vs Actual)		$0.00	$0.00	$0.00	$0.00
	Actual Income vs Actual Expense		$0.00	$0.00	$0.00	$0.00
Expenses						
Monthly recurring amount ($)	**Monthly Expense by category:**		$0.00	$0.00	$0.00	$0.00
	Activities					
	Allowance					
	Medical					
	Childcare					
	Clothing					
	School					
	Toys					
	Other					
	Planned Vs. Actual		$0.00	$0.00	$0.00	$0.00

If you're not into my spreadsheets, feel free to download one of the apps listed below and give that a go.

APPS THAT YOU'LL LOVE

Here they are in no particular order.

Apps for the US:

1. ***Mint*** – In the US, Mint is the oldest and best software to use. It connects to your bank accounts so you don't need to enter expenses manually. Mint is great for tracking past spending. I've not personally used it for this, but I've heard great things about it.

2. ***PocketGuard*** – Works like Mint and is easy to use. It also helps you locate potential savings on existing expenses such as utility bills.

3. ***Every Dollar*** – This is an excellent budget planning app. You input your expected income for the whole month, and it allows you to create a forecast.

4. ***YNAB*** – This is by far one of the most popular apps for budgeting, and for good reason. It also connects to your bank accounts. And you know those budgeting categories we talked about creating earlier? YNAB does exactly that. It allows you to create categories according to your needs and set customizable spending goals for each one. It also helps you become more mindful of your spending by allowing you to see trends in spending for each category. If you want to track what you've already spent, YNAB isn't for you. YNAB

only works with the money currently available in your bank account. So if you want to budget ahead for money that you don't yet physically have, it won't let you do that. It adopts a real-time, hands-on approach that forces you to choose your priorities and fund them only with the money you currently have. And yes, you have to pay for it. However, they offer a free year for students. You've probably just finished being a student and can't take them up on that offer. Typical, right? It's like warranties for electronic devices that expire a month before they break. For others who also aren't students (i.e., the rest of us), there is often a free trial period available. Regardless, consider this an investment in your financial future. I know, a coffee is more preferable, but this is also worth it. You're worth it.

Apps for the UK:

1. ***Emma*** – It highlights wasteful subscriptions, so that's a huge plus. You don't need *The New York Times, USA Today, The Guardian, The Telegraph, The Wall Street Journal,* AND *The Times.* They're all the same political rubbish, some with a left spin and some with a right. Regardless, it's all nonsense. I prefer a news source that comes with its own sandbox to bury your head in.

2. *Yolt* – It seamlessly connects to multiple accounts. Track spending across all of them in one easy-to-use dashboard. Their ad campaigns are about as boring as this book could have been, but don't be put off by that. Perhaps I should write their advertisements.

3. *Money Dashboard* – It's quite comprehensive like the previous two options. Take all three out for a trial run and see which one fits you best.

4. *Cleo* – It uses artificial intelligence to help you manage money. It's not my personal favorite, but you can play around with its resident chatbot, which is a lot of fun. It's also really easy to use. Hopefully there is no doomsday scenario where your AI bot starts stalking my AI bot and sends me flowers paid by your account. If that happens, you might want to uninstall the app.

AVOID THESE BUDGET BUSTERS

Here are some of the mistakes you want to avoid at all costs (Caldwell, 2020):

1. Not having a budget. Duh.
2. Guessing expenses instead of verifying them through bank statements.
3. Not tracking expenses each month.
4. Confusing wants with needs. You need food. You want a fancy restaurant meal.

5. Living like a monk. Cutting down on entertainment is important to help you reach your goals, but going from one extreme to another only leads to burnout. It is important to budget for fun; otherwise, the changes you make will not be sustainable.

ACTION PLAN – DAYS 7–9

- Determine if you are happy with the way you have prioritized your spending over the last three months, and decide what needs to change.
- Calculate your monthly expenses based on past spending.
- Decide on your budgeting method. Either download my toolkit from www.30daymoneyschool.com or install the app you want to use. If you decide on an app, take some time to run through introductory videos on how to use them.
- Create your spending plan in seven simple steps.
- Once you have set spending limits for each category, begin tracking your actual spending vs. your planned spending. You will need to update your spending limits and allocations as you work your way through the book and as we delve into more detail around savings, debt, and investment.

5

BEYOND THE PIGGY BANK – SAVING MONEY THE RIGHT WAY

"Too many people spend money they haven't earned, to buy things they don't want, to impress people that they don't like."

— WILL ROGERS

Raise a hand if you think saving money is tough. Raise another hand if you think buying a new pair of shoes is much easier. Now raise a third hand if you're not from planet Earth.

Of course, saving is tough. I used to earn a pretty decent salary but still found it incredibly easy to blow my paycheck each month. Maybe that's why I like *Gone with the Wind* so much. I could never understand where all the money went.

Studies show that 60% of Americans have less than $1,000 saved (Urosevic, 2020). This is a pretty alarming statistic when you consider that according to the United States Census Bureau, the median salary in the United States in 2019 was $68,703 (Semega et al., 2020). Where does all that money go? My advice to the United States Census Bureau is to put a small tracker on that money, hire a team of private investigators, and follow it wherever it takes them. I think it's in the public interest to expose, with photographs, where that money goes. Then we'll all know.

Unnecessary spending on wants is one explanation. I'd expect those photographs to include a sneaky trip to the casino where we could watch the money getting absolutely wasted, falling down drunk, photographed on a Friday night with some of *your* cash, too. In fact, when you created your own budget using the directions in the previous chapter, you might have found a shortfall. Your expenses were greater than your income.

There are other factors such as the rising cost of living. However, there are probably people you know who earn less than you and still manage to have enough money every month. How do they do it? It comes back to managing money using a budget. Think of it like those police officers who stand in the middle of the road directing traffic. They're pretty boring, but they keep all of you driving forward. And sometimes they dance, so it's not all bad.

Let's talk about savings and how you need to go about setting up everything correctly.

WHY YOU NEED TO SAVE MONEY

Once again, I'm not taking any chances. There might be a possibility that you're unaware of how important it is to save money. Let me write this very slowly so the message sinks in. It...is... really...important...to...save...money. That should do it, hey? Once you read about the advantages of saving money, you'll have no more doubts in your mind. Well, not about money, though you might still harbor a doubt or two about the Moon landings or whether the Earth really could be round.

Better Mental Health

If you're constantly worried about money and are trying to figure out where the cash to pay your next bill is going to come from, keep an eye on the delivery routes of the cash transit vans. There are some great ~~movies~~ documentaries that tell you how to knock them over and not get caught. Or do a budget—whichever is easier for you. Money is a central part of our lives, and not having control over it can put our mental health at risk. A study found that individuals suffering from depression and anxiety are three times more likely to be struggling with debt (Morin, 2019). Take care of your money now, and you'll be taking care of your mental health as well.

A healthy level of savings makes it much easier to cope with life and the problems it throws your way.

Better Financial Decisions

The very act of saving is a good financial decision. I know when you hear *saving*, you're probably thinking rescuing people from earthquake-damaged buildings. That's fine and all, but I remember making scrambled eggs the other day, and a raw egg rolled off the counter. How I managed to catch it, I don't know, but *that* was a legendary save. And before you start saying that's not a financial saving decision, that egg was worth at least $0.10.

When you start carrying out the right habits, your brain builds neural networks that enforce the good habit. Carry it out often enough and it becomes second nature to you. When was the last time you consciously racked your brain to figure out how to brush your teeth? You've done it so many times that you can do it with your eyes closed.

Start saving money, and it will produce a snowball effect on your financial habits. You'll develop even more good financial habits, and best of all, you'll have money at your disposal to put these habits into action. For example, you'll have a good amount of money saved up to invest and create assets.

Access to the Things You Love

Why are you reading this book? Sorry, that came off a bit harsh. But what I mean is there's soooo much good stuff to watch online from your favorite streaming service that I've got to ask why you're reading this book. You're certainly not reading it because you thought my name looked cool on the cover. You might say it's to learn how to manage money. Why do you want to manage your money well? Going even deeper, why do you want to earn more money in the first place? For most people, getting rich isn't about earning money. It's about using that money to buy access to the things they really love spending time on. Personally, not having to worry about money means I can spend more time with my family and travel the world. Do you think Bill Gates does a single thing during his day that he doesn't like? He's rich enough to hire someone to do it for him. Well, nearly everything. I don't think he keeps a butler in the john.

Money in the bank, via savings or assets, gives you freedom to spend your time exactly as you please. If you had a million bucks in the bank, would you ever listen to your knucklehead of a boss? Likely not! You'd probably be lying on a beach somewhere with your partner or friends.

Options, Options, Options

Savings in the bank give you options. I'm not talking about the kinds of options I just highlighted. I'm talking about financial options, the ability to invest in and create assets. You can own property, have a sizable investment account balance, or own a second home on an island somewhere. The choice is yours. You don't need to worry about opportunities passing you by because when you have money, opportunities will come to you. It's just how the world works.

Money Works for You

The rich don't work for money. They work for time freedom, and the less rich work for them. To achieve this, they earn money and put it to work. Whether it's through interest-earning investments or new businesses, money works overtime for them and creates even more money. This allows the rich to prioritize what they really want to do.

Contrast this with how a poor person has to live. Before I began my personal finance journey, I used to work more than 60 hours a week. I was constantly traveling over weekends for work. Once I began investing my money, I realized the importance of having your money work for you. I now earn twice what I used to but work far fewer hours.

Aim to save at least 20% of your income when you're starting out. If you're a student, that is going to be pretty tough. At that income level, every penny saved is a hard-core victory. You should be properly proud of yourself. Doing anything is better than doing nothing. Start saving now, and you'll start creating more wealth for yourself. Eventually, you can increase the percentage of your income you save and travel the path of financial freedom.

Banks offer products that can help you achieve your savings goals. The list below covers the most common savings instruments you can use.

1. *Regular savings accounts* – These accounts are offered by your bank and typically pay the lowest rate of interest. However, they're better than nothing. They're best used for cash you need in the very short term.

2. *High-yield savings accounts* – These savings accounts pay higher interest rates. However, a lot of them have investment minimums (so always check), and it might take a few days for any withdrawals to appear in your regular account.

3. *Certificates of Deposit* – CDs work much like high-yield accounts. They last for a fixed term, and you will be paid interest at the end of that term, along with receiving your deposit back. Early withdrawal attracts penalties.

4. *Goals-oriented savings* – Some banks offer savings accounts that help you plan your savings toward a goal such as a vacation or a big purchase. Contributing money from your budget to such accounts makes a lot of sense.

5. *Student savings* – Banks offer savings accounts

designed for students, with low minimum balances.
These accounts also have zero monthly fees. Check
with your bank for such accounts.

It's always helpful to study benchmarks to figure out where you
need to be. The table below indicates the ideal retirement
savings amount and emergency fund size you ought to have if
you are based in the US, depending on your age (how much you
should have in savings at each age) (Goldberg, 2020).

Age	Retirement Saving Goal	Emergency Saving Goal
30	$74,082	$14,114 to $28,228
40	$289,743	$17,800 to $35,599
50	$656,196	$18,847 to $37,694
60	$706,736	$16,553 to $33,106

Table 1: Savings Goals for the US.

Note: Retirement savings goals are based on Fidelity's recom-
mendations using data in the U.S. Bureau of Labor Statistics'
Consumer Expenditure Survey, 2018. Emergency savings goals
are calculated using the average annual expenditure mean for
that age group in that same survey. The monthly average is
multiplied by three and six months to get the range (how much
you should have in savings at each age) (Goldberg, 2020).

WHAT TO SAVE FOR

There are many expenses you're going to encounter in life. The ones I'm going to highlight are just the ones you can be certain to encounter. I'm reminded of the guy married for 50 years who was asked if he remembered how much his wedding cost. "I don't know," he replied. "I'm still paying for it." Life will throw you a few unexpected expenses, so it's critical that you have enough money in the bank to pay for them. Here are the ones you definitely need to plan for.

Debt Repayment

You cannot become financially free while carrying debt. Have you ever tried getting somewhere quickly by hopping on one leg? Not only will you look ridiculous, you have close to no chance of getting there quickly. This is what it's like to try to become financially free while carrying loads of debt. You're going to amass debt as you lead your life, whether you like it or not.

It is possible to consciously reduce your debt burden, but debt isn't fully avoidable. You'll have to assume debt in order to build assets and boost your net worth. To repay debt, you need savings.

Emergency Fund

I've covered this in the previous chapter. You need to have at least six months worth of expenses saved in your bank account

(Cothern, 2020). This money should be liquid, which refers to money that is easily accessible, preferably instantly. For example, money held in a CD is not fully liquid. You can access it, but you'll have to pay early withdrawal fees. Savings account balances are liquid, and that's where your immediate emergency cash needs to be.

Retirement

Retirement seems far away, but it pays to start as early as possible. Here's an interesting question. What do you think it takes to become a millionaire? Do you need to start a hot startup? Do you need to be a whiz at something extraordinary? The answer is much more boring than that. Here's what it takes:

- $1,000 per month
- invested in the stock market
- for 25 years

That's it. We'll talk about *how* to do this in later chapters. For now, ask yourself-can you rustle up $1,000 per month? If you're 25 years old now, you could have a million by the time you're 50. That's 10 years before most people start thinking of retiring. The reason making a million is straightforward is because of the power of compounding. To better understand compounding, think of a snowball rolling down a hill.

At first, your snowball is about as big as your fist. However, it collects a little snow every inch as it proceeds downhill, and soon, it's as big as a large rock. It continues rolling downhill, and soon, it's as big as a boulder. If it keeps rolling downhill, it'll eventually assume avalanche-like proportions. Compounding requires just two things: consistency and time. Incorporate both of these into your investments and financial habits, and you'll end up with a million before you know it!

Repairs

You might be living in a dorm right now, but take it from me, in a few years you'll want to move into a more adult-like living space. Seems crazy, I know. Most people eventually buy a home and a car, and there are two things that both of them do: break down. A car can have a flat tire or a slipping transmission, and a home might need some plumbing repairs.

You need some cash in the bank to pay for these repairs.

Buying a Home

For most of you, there will come a time when you'll want to buy your own house. You'll want to have something that's yours, where you don't need permission to put up some shelves or change the wallpaper. A house purchase is typically financed. This is banking-speak for taking out a loan. In order to get a loan, you need to pay some money up front and then pay monthly installments. If you want to borrow money to buy a house in the US, you'll usually need to pay between 3% and 20% of its value up front. If you are putting down less than 20%, you'll need to pay for Private Mortgage Insurance (PMI) as well, at least until you have 20% equity in the home. The higher your down payment is, the less you'll pay on your mortgage monthly installments. Keep that in mind when making a decision.

You'll also need another 3% of the overall value to pay for what are called closing costs. There are many professionals involved in a home financing deal, and those folks need to get paid. Prospective homebuyers often forget about closing costs. For example, if the house is worth $150,000 and you're putting down 20% up front, you'll need $34,500 saved up.

Buying a Vehicle

Purchasing a vehicle is an expense that will hit you in the face right when you enter the adult world. You might be tempted to buy a Ferrari or a Rolls Royce, like the ones you see in Drake's videos, but respectfully, those cars are terrible for your finances. A car is a liability because it decreases in value every day you own it. Yet they cost a lot, and you might be forced to take out a loan to pay for it.

My advice is to buy the cheapest and most reliable car you can find and pay for it in full. You'll lose the least amount of money by doing this. If you can't find such a car, you'll need to save money for a down payment. Nearly every loan requires a down payment. Save money starting now so you won't have to rely on a beater to get you to and from work.

Entrepreneurial Ambitions

Everyone has creative ideas. At some point, you'll want to either create a new product or invest in a business that can generate income on the side. I'll discuss these ideas in more detail later in this book. No matter what your idea is, you need cash to invest. It's close to impossible to make a business work without investing money in it. Even online businesses require advertising, and this means you need to spend money. It's a lot easier to generate a second income when you have cash to invest in creating it.

Little Luxuries

Sometimes life can be a bit too much. It'll make you want to curl into a ball and have someone pet you. Unfortunately, you're an adult, so no one is going to do that. The best option you have is to pamper yourself with whatever strikes your fancy. Wouldn't it be nice to have enough cash to splurge on ridiculous things without having to worry about blowing your budget? Everyone can use a little pampering now and then.

Caring for Yourself and Your Family

Your family's and your health is a priority, and you should never take that for granted. Always prepare for the unexpected. I'll discuss health insurance later in this book. For now, understand that you'll need to set some money aside for this.

THE FIVE-STEP SAVINGS PRIORITIZATION LADDER

There's so much money to save, so where should you begin? That is where the savings prioritization ladder comes in. No matter what your current situation is, you'll be able to figure out where your savings allocations need to go.

Step One – Emergency Fund

An emergency fund is where it all begins. Call it a rainy day fund, a financial freedom fund, or the $balla$ fund; this money should be equal to your living expenses for six months at the very least. Place this money in a high-yield savings account. Make sure you have easy access to this money and that you won't be hit with fees if you withdraw it.

Some online banks have a minimum balance requirement, so don't opt for the highest interest paying option automatically. Choose an account where your cash is the most liquid.

Step Two – Retirement Savings

The second step is to divert money into a retirement account such as an Individual Retirement Account (IRA) or a 401(k).

There's a caveat to this, however. If you're carrying any amount of high-interest debt such as a student loan, or credit card debt, you should only invest money in an employer-matched 401(k) at this stage. I'll talk more about this in Chapter 11, but what it means is that your employer may match the contributions you make to this account, up to a certain amount (usually a fixed percentage of your annual salary). If you don't take advantage of this, you're essentially leaving free money on the table.

Here's an easy way for you to understand what to do:

Do you have debt? If the answer is yes, invest only in an employer-matched 401(k) at this point. The rest of your savings should go toward debt repayment (see Step 3).

If the answer is no, invest in an employer matched 401(k) first and then an IRA. These are tax-advantaged accounts so it makes sense to max these out first, before investing elsewhere.

Step Three – Repay High-Interest Debt and Start to Invest

Chapter 6 will deal with the methods of repaying high-interest debt. Briefly, you need to pay your debts off as quickly as you can. This is especially the case with credit card debt. The average interest rate on credit cards in America is 16.05% (Dilworth, 2020). No one can become financially free by borrowing money at those rates. Student loan debt also comes with high principals. Pay this off as quickly as you can and on a priority basis.

Should you invest in stocks or bonds while carrying debt? For most people, the answer is no. However, if you're young, you can afford to take a few risks and take advantage of compounding. It takes time to get a hang of investing, and it's better to start sooner rather than later. While the priority is to always pay your high-interest debt off first, wherever possible make small contributions toward your investment accounts. As mentioned earlier, your 401(k) and IRA's are tax-advantaged accounts so max those out before investing elsewhere. Read, learn, and practice. We'll cover investing basics in Chapter 11.

Step Four – Savings for the Next Year

This money is equal to your expenses for your wants for the next year. Place this money in a high-yield savings account and use it for home refurbishing, car purchases, and vacations planned for the next 12 months.

Step Five – Long-Term Savings

Long-term savings can include paying for a wedding, buying a home, and so on. Since these are considerable expenses, you are better off funding these using a long-term investment strategy since it will have a much better rate of return than even the best savings accounts. This is all covered in Chapter 11.

To help you visualize this, here's a lovely picture of my savings prioritization ladder. See how happy the girl is at the top of the ladder? That could be you. Sure, she needs a better dress and the shoes could do with some attention, but that's the point, isn't it? She's conserving money on the less important things to get where she wants to go. This is the book that will take you there. This picture is a great way to remind yourself of what your savings priorities should be. Hit me up if you want a free print-able copy for your ladder (you know you want to).

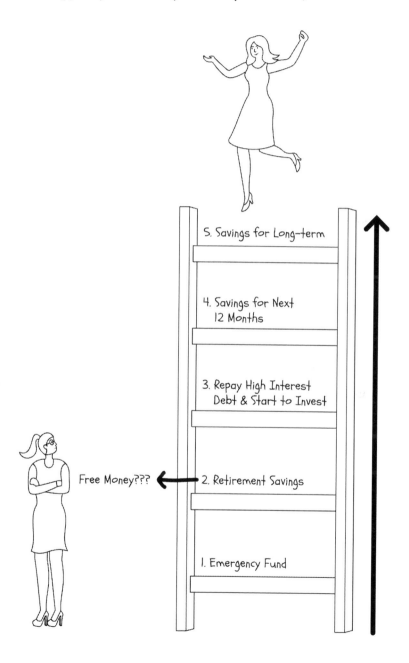

5. Savings for Long-term

4. Savings for Next 12 Months

3. Repay High Interest Debt & Start to Invest

Free Money??? ← 2. Retirement Savings

1. Emergency Fund

SETTING SAVINGS GOALS

My beautifully orchestrated ladder above gives you a good idea of what savings goals to prioritize and where to store the money so you don't get tempted by it. The best way to make these goals real and attainable for you is to write down the amount of money you need to save and then open the appropriate savings accounts.

Start contributing money toward it, and if possible, automate your transfer to that account. You can set up a standing instruction that transfers a percentage of your paycheck to the savings account every month. Other automation solutions include round-up apps. These apps round your expenditures to the latest dollar and put those pennies into an investment account.

For example, if you paid $4.98 for a cup of coffee, a round-up app transfers two cents into an investment account. You're unlikely to notice two-cent deficits, but over time, it adds up. You can open multiple savings accounts to easily track your progress. Again, it doesn't matter whether you're saving just a few cents or whether you're saving thousands. Everything is progress, so start taking action.

Below is a template savings tracker you can use to help you document and visualize your savings goals. As an example, I've populated some of the rows on behalf of my friend Harry, and I'll walk you through that in a minute. You can find the digital and printable version of this tracker at www.30daymoneyschool.com.

Harry has an annual salary of $60,000. For the purposes of keeping this example really simple, I will ignore taxes. That means Harry makes $5,000 per month. After expenses and wants, Harry is left with $2,500 for savings, debt repayment, and investing. If we take away his wants, Harry's actual monthly expenditure is $2,000. That means he needs to save $12,000 for his emergency fund. That will be Harry's top priority. However, Harry also owes $2,400 on his credit card. And Harry's employer matches his 401(k) contributions, so he doesn't want to miss out on that.

In Harry's case, he doesn't have any other high-interest debt. He also doesn't have any other pressing savings goals—no upcoming weddings or refurbishments that can't be postponed. It is January, and Harry's New Year's resolution is to have a more structured savings plan. Therefore, Harry decides to set his short- to medium-term goals as follows: (1) save up for emergency fund within six months, (2) start contributing minimum amounts to 401(k) to avoid losing out on free money, (3) pay off credit card within six months, and (4) once the six months are over, have a complete emergency fund and no high-interest debt. At that point, Harry will have $2,500 to contribute to his 401(k) and other investment opportunities. Since the maximum amount you can contribute to a 401(k) in a year is $19,500 (we touch on this later), Harry will start putting

$1,625 per month into his 401(k) and the balance toward other investments. Since IRA's are also tax-advantaged accounts, Harry decides to contribute the balance toward his IRA.

You see, every individual's situation is different. However, the ladder above and the tracker below will help you set some effective short-term and long-term savings goals. They also serve as a useful reminder for what you want to achieve in life. If your long-term goals are super ambitious (e.g., you're saving up for a $20,000 trip to a private island in Maldives), you can start planning now. Find a way to increase your income, reduce your expenses, and put more money into your savings.

	Savings Goal (in order of priority)	Total Amount To Save ($)	Start Date	End Date (Deadline)	Amount To Save Each Month ($)	Account To Open	Open & Standing order Set Up (Y/N)	Goal Achieved (Y/N)
Short–Medium Term Goals	1. Emergency Fund	$12,000 (Average monthly expenses x 6 months)	1–Jan–21	1–Jun–21	$2,000	HYSA (high yield savings account)	Y	
	2. Retirement (Employer matched 401(k))	$600	1–Jan–21	1–Jun–21	$100	401(k)	Y	
	3. High-interest debt	$2,400	1–Jan–21	1–Jun–21	$400	N/A–automatic transfer from checking account	Y	
	4. Retirement (Employer matched 401(k))	$19,500	1–Jun–21	1–Jun–22	$1,625	401(k)	Y	
	5. Investing in Roth or Traditional IRA	$10,500	1–Jun–21	1–Jun–22	$875	TBC.. Harry will decide once he reaches Chapter 11	N	

A good way to use the tracker is to work your way backward. Let's say Harry wants to buy a house in the next five to seven years. He will need a down payment of around $125,000. If he starts saving for this in June 2022, he'll need to save approximately $2,000 per month to reach that goal within five years. Harry knows the best way to achieve that is to invest his savings and let compound interest do its magic. Now Harry can work out how much he needs to invest each month in order to get the return he needs.

	Savings Goal (in order of priority)	Total Amount To Save ($)	Start Date	End Date (Deadline)	Amount To Save Each Month ($)	Account To Open	Open & Standing order Set Up (Y/N)	Goal Achieved (Y/N)
Long-Term Goals	1. Buy a house	$125,000	1-Jun-22	1-Jun-27	$2,000	TBC_Harry will decide once he reaches Chapter 11	N	

APPS TO HELP YOU SAVE

If you're in the US, here are your best options for apps to help you save (Tierney, 2020):

1. **Digit** – This is the easiest app to use. You can calculate what you can realistically save and set it aside. You'll receive a 1% bonus every three months. Free money!
2. **Qapital** – This is a savings and round-up app in one package. Set goals and sweep spare change into an investment account.
3. **Acorns** – This is the OG round-up app. It gives you a variety of investment options. If you're in college, you can use it for free for four years.

Here are some of the best options if you live in the UK (Burrows, 2020):

1. *Plum* – Best for large savings targets. It will help you analyze your spending and set savings goals.
2. *Tandem* – A great and easy-to-use round-up app.
3. *Chip* – This is an automated savings solution and uses AI to help you save money.

ACTION PLAN – DAYS 10–12

Here are the next steps you need to take to implement your savings plan:

- Do your research! Look up some of the savings account and app options. Look at those I've listed and some I have not. Make a list of their features, and choose the right one.
- Set your savings goals according to the prioritization ladder.
- Use the savings goals tracker above to make note of progress as you work through this list.
- Open an account, and put some money into it. Even if it's a measly penny, do it! Set up an automatic transfer with your bank.
- If you are using my budgeting toolkit from Chapter 4, enter your savings allocations in the Forecast tab. If you're like Harry and your goals will change after six months, simply adjust these allocations as you go along.

- You might look at the amount of money you need to save and get discouraged. This is focusing on the negative. Stay positive and pat yourself on the back for taking action. Every cent you save counts.

"It is not necessary to do extraordinary things to get extraordinary results."

— WARREN BUFFETT

6

STEER CLEAR OF THE RABBIT HOLE OF DEBT – HOW TO DEAL WITH DEBT AND MANAGE IT WELL

"The only man who sticks closer to you in adversity than a friend, is a creditor."

— UNKNOWN

I don't know who came up with the above quote, but boy, is it true. Don't ask me how I know that. Let's just say if you're ever facing any financial troubles, at the very least you can count on your bank to be calling you. Anyway, moving on....

What is debt? Easy-peasy, lemon-squeezy—we all know the answer to that. It's money we owe to someone else. But debt as a part of personal finance is heavily misunderstood. On one extreme there are those who think borrowed money is their money and they can spend it as they wish. On the other extreme are those who think debt is the root of all evil. I've been at both ends of the spectrum, and I can tell you that neither is correct. Just because you *can* spend $2,000 on a credit card doesn't mean you should. At the same time, debt is not universally bad and *can* be used strategically to boost long-term wealth. However, being able to use debt strategically requires an in-depth understanding of how it works.

Ever had someone give you constructive criticism? As a college student, I didn't take constructive criticism too well. I thought it was just a polite way of teachers telling me I suck. Maybe it was. Who knows TBH? But the dictionary definition of constructive is something having or intended to have a useful or beneficial purpose. That's what I call constructive debt, a form of debt intended to be used to your advantage.

Before I go into that, I'd like you to ask yourself a simple question. Are you in debt? If the answer is yes, know that some debt can be used to your advantage and some should be paid off immediately. Your task in this part of the book is to figure out which type of debt you have and to establish whether your debt is constructive debt or not. If you don't have any debt, I want you to ask yourself, "How can I start using debt to my advantage?"

The money-wise, debt-savvy peeps (like *me*, if I can say so myself) use debt as leverage. Let's say I want to invest in a property with 10% of my own money and 90% from the bank = 100% of required finance. If the property's price goes up by just 10% to 110% of the original and I pay the bank back its 90%, then I'm left with my original 10% + another 10%. I've doubled my money even though the price has only gone up 10%. But that's the debt lever—a small investment can leverage a big return. However, if the price goes down by only 10%, I lose all my money. As always, there's risk and reward. Did you know that as of 2018, the average American owes $90,460 in outstanding debt ("American Consumer Debt Statistics," 2020)? That is higher than the average American's yearly salary. However, I can guarantee that the average American's debt of $90,460 is not being used that way. It's most likely composed of vehicle and credit card debt, not financial investments.

Back to my point about risk and reward. The key to understanding whether an investment is a good risk or not is to understand the likelihood of failure of the investment. Big banks have massive departments focused just on risk, so don't worry your little brains about that too much. All you need to do for now is realize that risk is a key driver of success, and then do your best to take it into account.

So before we discuss the various methods of debt reduction and debt payoff, we need to understand this:

1. The different types of debt
2. The risks they pose vs. their potential reward

We've already covered most of these definitions, but in case you didn't do your homework (tut, tut!), I'll go over them briefly. There are three main elements to all forms of debt:

- **Principal** – the amount of money you borrowed
- **Interest** – the money you pay for the privilege of borrowing money from someone; the profit your lender makes by loaning you money
- **Term** – the length of the loan. Your lender will devise a monthly repayment plan that will last for a term. Your monthly payment will include principal and interest repayments.

Some forms of debt, such as mortgages, have lengthy terms. Others, such as credit card debt, have variable terms and depend on how long you take to repay the principal. The longer you carry unpaid principal on a variable term loan, the more interest you'll end up paying. That's all really. Let's move on.

THE RISKS AND REWARDS OF DEBT

Debt can be extremely useful for increasing wealth. However, borrowing money from others always means they want their money back, with interest. As a form of insurance, the organization lending the money may require you to put up an asset (called collateral) in case your plans don't go as you intended and you can't repay the loan as you expected. They can then sell this asset to raise the money they lent you. It should be obvious that taking on debt may mean losing an asset, so debt should only be considered with the benefits it brings and in light of the asset you might lose.

Constructive Debt

Mortgages

A mortgage is a fancy name for a loan to buy a home. Mortgages are the most common form of debt because people use them to buy property. Property ownership can boost your net worth considerably, and income can be earned from a property you own and rent out. The point at which to consider buying property in order to earn rental income is when that monthly rental income offsets the mortgage payment and all expenses. Remember to account for periods of no income when the property is vacant.

For example, if you can earn $1,000 per month in rent and if maintenance costs are $500 and your mortgage payment is $500, you don't need to pay out of pocket to own the property. It pays for itself. Nice, huh?

Now if you have a mortgage and live at the property, you still own the property. Having a debt against it doesn't change the legal position of your ownership. However, if you miss your monthly payments, the bank can kick you out. That's called a foreclosure. You'll lose all the money you've previously paid, and the bank will sell the property to someone else.

Borrowing money and choosing to live in that property can be a good move, assuming the value of the property increases over time. And with every mortgage payment you make, you are building equity in your home. The dictionary definition for home equity is the amount of money someone would receive if they sold their house after paying off the mortgage. I think that is important to get your head around, so let's use an example.

Imagine you purchased a house for $300,000, put 20% down, and took out a loan to cover the remaining amount. In this example, your home equity is equal to 20% of the property's value (i.e., $60,000). You owe the lender $240,000.

Make sense? Being able to build equity in your home is a primary reason mortgages are considered "constructive" debt.

There are two ways to build home equity:

1. Make your loan payments on time. Reduce the amount you owe to the lender, and your home equity increases.
2. Pray that house prices continue to rise. Let's assume that the economy is booming and house prices double. Your property is now worth $600,000 on the market. However, you still owe the lender only $240,000. That means your equity in the house has increased. House value ($600,000) – borrowed amount ($240,000) = $360,000, which is yours. That $360,000 is 60% of the total property value. You're killin' it!

A home is considered a milestone purchase, and most people want to own their own living space. But make sure you can cover your monthly payments so you aren't at risk of losing your home. Mortgages offer a great pathway to homeowner-ship, but as the Great Recession (2007–2009) showed us, it's not foolproof. Home prices can fall, and mortgage debt is a serious burden that can bankrupt you if circumstances turn against you.

Use online calculators to determine how much you can borrow, and don't overextend yourself. In general, most lenders follow the 28/36 rule to determine your affordability for a mortgage. I won't go into detail about this for fear I might lose you to extreme boredom, but it's helpful to take a look at it yourself prior to applying for a mortgage. You can try out the calculator at: https://www.omnicalculator.com/finance/28-36-rule.

Small Business Loans

Small business loans can be an excellent way to boost earnings and make more money, provided the underlying business plan is solid. Taking on debt for an unrealistic expansion is just silly, and there are too many corporate failures where the debt didn't match the possibilities.

That said, when life gives you lemons, make lemonade. If you own a lemonade stand and it's doing well, it makes sense to expand. (True story: I had a very successful lemonade stand at age 9). Let's look at an example.

You're making $10 a month in profit. Mom and Dad are paying for the lemons, sugar, and plastic cups, so luckily you don't have any expenses. However, you want to expand and set up another lemonade stand that Mom and Dad aren't willing to pay for. A new stand costs $500, so it's going to take you 50 months to save up for it with the money you're currently making. However, if you open a second stand, you could double your monthly profit to $20.

With 1 Stand

Monthly Profit	Cost of New Stand	Time Required to Save
$10	$500	50 months

The solution in this case is to borrow $500 from the bank. Let's say the bank affixes a monthly payment of $5 to this loan. You open your new lemonade stand and are earning $20 per month less the loan payment of $5 per month. Your monthly profit is now $15, which is a 50% increase from before ($10). That is called smart borrowing.

With 2 Stands

Revenue	Expenses (Money Owed to Bank)	Monthly Profit
$20	$5	$15

Let's say you're not great at the lemonade business and are actually losing $5 per month. For some strange reason, you think opening a second stand will make you some money, and you decide to borrow $500. The second stand makes $5 per month, which is far less than you projected. You now have a loss of $5 on one stand and a profit of $5 on another. Your business is breaking even. However, you now have to make monthly loan payments of $5 to the bank.

Total Revenue (Stand 1 + Stand 2)	Expenses (Money Owed to the Bank)	Monthly Income
$0	$5	-$5

As a result, you have a loss of $5 and also the burden of owing money to the bank. If you fail to pay this amount, you'll lose your business. This was not the case before you borrowed money. This is a classic example of how to use small business loans *unwisely*.

Student Loans

Student loans have recently become a hot topic, and deservedly so. I mean, who *doesn't* want the college experience? Ramen noodles and booze, messy dorm rooms, lack of sleep, and -$125 in the bank account—sounds like a real treat, doesn't it? Jokes aside, I wouldn't trade those years for anything. I managed to graduate in one piece, find an adult job, and locate an adult-like place to live in. What I didn't realize, though, is how long I'd be holding on to my student loan debt.

The majority of people view education as an asset worth investing in. And I agree. But should you borrow money to fund it? At the risk of sounding controversial, that depends. Borrowing money by default is almost never the correct choice.

In some fields, great value is placed on a paper degree from a traditional, well-respected college. There are also many perks to attending traditional institutions, such as helping you form a strong professional network early on in your career. And with certain professions such as medicine, college is the only option. That is why I call it constructive debt. It has the potential to bring you real rewards in the long term.

However, the world is a very different place today. There is an abundance of knowledge available online. There are online university courses that are almost as good as the traditional ones. If you're studying engineering, you can earn an Associate's degree in two years (or less if you opt for AP or dual credit classes in high school), earn a salary, and use that to fund a Bachelor's degree. This is an increasingly common route for students looking to fund Master's and doctoral degrees.

So I urge you to think about this: How much is your degree really worth? And is it a smart investment? A smart investment gives you a good return. Let's say you're paying $25,000 per year for four years to study computer science; that's a total of $100,000—plus interest. How long will it take to pay this back? Online calculators can help you figure that out. And what financial position do you expect to be in at that time? Look up salary expectations for your career path. Compare that to the position you'll be in after the same amount of time without having a degree. That should help you make a decision.

Research other options, too. For example, if you're thinking of computer science, Tesla doesn't require college degrees, and neither does Google. You can learn programming online for a lot less than the cost of college tuition.

It comes down to your personal situation and career goals. Ask yourself:

- Is a traditional college degree necessary for my career path?
- If the answer is yes, are there alternative ways to fund it?

And remember, not all investments are hard and fast and based on numbers. Consider all the intangible benefits of college life, too—great friends, a wealth of new perspectives that may challenge you in healthy ways, and delaying the inevitable drudgery of being a full-fledged adult. I've given you the lowdown. The decision is yours.

Debt to Avoid

Unless you want to be on Santa's naughty list next year, start paying off the types of debt discussed below. They involve borrowing money to purchase depreciating assets. Such assets do not produce income and actually decrease your net worth over time. Basically, they bleed you dry.

Credit card debt

It's so easy to spend money on a credit card. And there's absolutely no judgment here. When I first got one, I was mesmerized by this shiny piece of plastic giving me access to all the shoes in the world; that is, until I was broke and had to sell those shoes. Ha! Anyway, credit card companies require a minimum payment each month, normally a small amount or a percentage of the amount you owe (whichever is larger). What tends to happen is that we get a credit card, make the minimum payments, give ourselves a pat on the back, and go to sleep peacefully on a bed of designer shoes (or a super-expensive mattress). Your choice. But we forget that the average interest rate on a credit card is around 17%. That's about 1.4% per month. If you only make the minimum payment, you'll help the credit card company achieve two goals: (1) they get some money coming in from you each month and like the cash flow, and (2) they get to add their ridiculous interest to the largest possible part of the amount owing. Lucky them. Not so lucky you. Let's see how damaging this is by looking at a simple example.

- Meet Jake and Amy. Both have been less than judicious with their credit card borrowing, and both owe $10,000 on their respective cards at 17% interest per year. Their minimum monthly payments are $300. Jake and Amy have come to their senses and have decided to pay off their debts.

- Jake looks at his budget and realizes he can allocate $400 toward paying off this debt. Using the calculator at https://calcxml.com/calculators/how-long-will-it-take-to-pay-off-my-credit-card, he realizes he can pay off this debt in 32 months. That's more than two and a half years.

- Amy uses the same calculator and realizes that if she can cut down on her wants and other less-than-desirable expenses, she can allocate $1,000 per month toward this debt. As a result, she'll pay off her debt in less than a year.

- She'll pay just $860 in interest, whereas Jake will pay $2,432 in interest. That is what you're paying for carrying an outstanding balance on your credit card.

- Carrying loan balances for as long as Jake does will result in damage to his credit score. We'll talk about that in more detail later on.

Credit card debt is very rarely constructive. On rare occasions (e.g., credit cards with a 0% transfer fee and a 0% interest rate), adding debt to a credit card can be a really good tactic. Likewise, using credit cards to collect rewards such as air miles is also pretty neat. And in some situations such as renting a car, the rental company doesn't accept debit cards. The company relies on the credit card company to chase you down for any outstanding debt if you run off with or damage their car. The bottom line is this: get a credit card but limit charging anything on it to a small amount that you can pay off in full each month for the sole purpose of establishing a better credit score.

Personal loans

Banks and lenders allow you to borrow money from them to put toward personal expenses. These loans are often taken out during times of emergency, but their interest rates are exorbitant. Avoid, avoid, avoid.

Payday loans

These are short-term loans provided by private lenders, usually to cover immediate or urgent cash requirements until you receive your next paycheck. They are also a means of committing financial suicide. Borrow enough of this kind of money and you'll be saddled with a lifetime of debt.

Vehicle loans

Vehicles depreciate over time, and as a result, you may owe more on your loan than what the car is worth. That new car smell really isn't worth it. Trust me. If you absolutely can't do without a car, make it a priority to save up and buy a second-hand one. If temptation hits, remember that all a car really does is take you from A to B. There are also ways to monetize your vehicle and have it pay for itself. Renting it to an Uber driver or using it for Carvertise can help you generate income. If this isn't practical for you, think about pursuing a second job as a delivery driver. If you need a car ASAP and an auto loan is the only option available to you, minimize your debt as much as possible.

Of all these, credit card debt is perhaps the easiest to avoid. As long as you pay your balance off in full every month, there's no risk of falling into a debt trap. Remember, the credit card company only cares about profit. As far as they're concerned, they'd prefer you remained in debt forever. They're definitely on the naughty list.

CREDIT HISTORY AND SCORES

Have you seen that *Black Mirror* episode where everyone walks around being super fake—nice to everyone and rating each other? The woman in that episode starts out as a 4.3, drops to a 2.7, and ends up having her life ruined. While our current world isn't as dystopian, your credit score and report function exactly as the rating system does in that episode. It quantifies you as a person. Go low enough on that scale, and everything becomes more expensive.

If your credit is poor, you'll pay more interest. And you won't be offered certain financial products because you're deemed too risky. For example, people with great credit receive credit card offers that give them a ton of freebies. These cards are never offered to those with poor credit. And if you have bad credit, you're likely seen as an employment risk. Want to start up a business? You'll have difficulty getting a business loan. Landlords may not rent to you, and you probably won't qualify for a mortgage. In summary, banks, landlords, mortgage lenders, and employers will all look at your credit score to determine your level of financial responsibility. So it's best to keep it in check.

And no, this doesn't mean you should avoid borrowing money altogether. The only thing worse than bad credit is no credit. You need to navigate the world of credit intelligently.

Understanding Credit Scores

Your entire financial life boils down to a number—the Fair, Isaac and Company (FICO) score. There is a second number—the VantageScore—but it isn't used as widely. FICO is a data analytics company that monitors credit reports and histories and uses them to come up with a number that reflects a person's credit-worthiness.

While the exact algorithm they use is unknown, there are five broad categories of data that influence your overall score (What's in my FICO scores?). See the chart below.

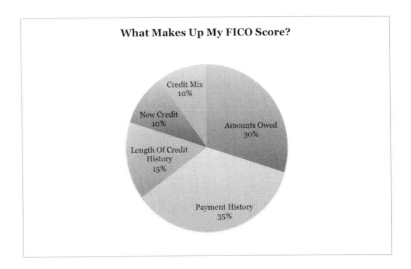

What Makes Up My FICO Score?

Credit Mix 10%
New Credit 10%
Amounts Owed 30%
Length Of Credit History 15%
Payment History 35%

- Payment history is the most important factor. It tells lenders whether or not you make payments on time.
- Amounts owed tell lenders how much of your available credit you are using. Your ratio of money owed to credit available is known as your credit utilization rate. If you are heavily dependent on credit, your credit utilization rate is high, and that's not a good sign.
- Length of credit history tells lenders how long your credit accounts have been open.
- Credit mix tells lenders how many different types of credit you have and how well you can manage them (e.g., credit cards, student loans, mortgages, etc.).

- New credit tells lenders how many credit accounts are new or recently opened. It also tells them how many credit checks were made. When you apply for new credit, lenders check your credit report. That is called a hard inquiry and shows up on the report.

An overall score greater than 670 is considered good. The maximum score you can attain is 850. If you have a score greater than 800, you can expect red carpet treatment from a bank or lender.

No one *really* knows how the final score is calculated behind the scenes. But if you follow the principles for good debt management that I've outlined in this chapter, you'll be just fine.

For my UK peeps, things are a bit different. There is no FICO equivalent in the UK, but credit scores do exist. There are three agencies, and each one has different scales to define good or bad. These three agencies—Equifax, Experian, and TransUnion —are in the US as well, and they're the ones that provide credit report data to FICO. Here are the numbers that are relevant to the UK ("What Is a Good or Average Credit Score?"):

Condition	Experian	Equifax	TransUnion
Fair	721-880	380-419	566-603
Good	881-960	420-465	604-627
Excellent	961-999	466-700	628-710

Table 1: Credit Score Ranges in the UK

In the US, each person is entitled to one free credit report per year. You can request it directly from your credit card provider. Note that your credit report doesn't include your credit score. Instead, your report lists all your active and prior credit accounts along with their payment statuses. Examining your credit report each year and looking out for any mistakes is important. You can dispute items on the report with the credit reporting agencies. Top tip: Don't dispute errors online. The more traditional approach of sending a letter to the credit bureau is more effective. Why? Because there's a paper trail, and written disputes are handled with more caution than those submitted online. The online forms are also a bit restrictive in the options they provide, making it harder to explain your individual situation. According to the FCRA (Fair Credit Reporting Act), the credit bureau must respond to any disputes within 30 days ("Consumer Reports: What Information Furnishers Need to Know"). If they don't respond, the item must be deleted from your credit reports.

MYTHBUSTERS: 5 MYTHS ABOUT CREDIT SCORES

Myth #1: If I don't have any credit card debt, my credit score will be good.

You need open and active accounts in order to build credit. You can build your credit with just mortgages and student loan debt, but remember that your FICO score is 10% credit mix. That means having a variety of credit types helps your score. Having a credit card and using it responsibly make building credit much easier.

Myth #2: I need to carry a credit card balance to build credit.

Actually, you need to do the exact opposite. Carrying a balance on your credit card just means you're paying ridiculous amounts in interest each month. And it doesn't do you any good. Yes, you need to use your credit card regularly in order to build up a solid payment history. But all that means is devoting a few small purchases to a designated credit card and paying that balance off immediately. That way you'll utilize credit (without paying interest), and your credit score will receive a boost.

Myth #3: I should cancel any credit cards I'm not using.

Uh, no. When you cancel a credit card, you lose its credit line. If you are carrying any credit card balances, that can make your credit utilization go up. And credit utilization accounts for 30% of your FICO score ("What Is a Credit Utilization Rate?"). Not good. For example, if your credit limit across all credit cards is $20,000 and if you have an unpaid balance of $1,000, your credit usage is (1,000/20,000), or 5%. Let's say you shut down a few cards and your credit limit is now $5,000. Overnight, your credit usage has gone up to 20%. Keep your old credit card accounts open even after you've paid off their balances so you still have their available credit and payment history.

Myth #4: Checking my report will hurt my credit score.

Do you like your eggs hard-boiled or soft and gooey? Don't roll your eyes at me; it's a relevant question. You see, there are two kinds of inquiries: hard and soft. When you apply for a credit card or a loan, your bank or lender checks your credit report, and that counts as a hard inquiry, which does affect your credit score. But when you check your own credit report, that's a soft inquiry that will not affect your credit score.

Myth #5: I've got lots of money, so my credit score should be great.

Sorry, pal. Your income, savings, and assets don't factor into your credit score. If you have tons of cash lying in the bank but you've never borrowed money before, your credit score could still be low.

BUILDING GOOD CREDIT

To summarize, here are seven ways to boost your credit score:

1. Borrow money, but handle it sensibly.
2. Make payments on time each month.

3. Pay your credit card in full each month.

4. Maintain a low utilization rate; don't max out the balance on your credit card just because you can.

5. Don't close down old credit cards.

6. Avoid making lots of new credit applications at once unless it's absolutely necessary.

7. Keep an eye on your credit report, and look for any errors.

If you're a student, I'm sure building good credit isn't at the top of your priority list right now. And I hate to be the one to break it to you, but adulting ain't easy. The more you prep for it now, the better off you'll be once you graduate.

Get your hands on a student credit card, use it minimally, and pay it off on time. Designate one purchase to it every month, and pay it off fully, immediately. You can also apply for secured credit cards. With these cards, you'll have to pay a refundable deposit, and your credit limit is fixed at the amount of money you pay as a deposit.

On another note, be good with your bills. While your utility bills don't usually impact your credit score, if you manage to miss a few payments and get passed on to a collection agency, credit bureaus are likely to find out. And it may be difficult to find another utility provider in the future. Just be sensible, kids.

We'll talk about student loan payments in a bit, but making some payments on your loan while you're still in school is a smart move. Not only does it help with your credit score but it will make things much easier for you when you graduate.

Another idea is to become an authorized user of someone else's credit card. Under this system, the bank issues the other person a credit card with your name on it and holds them liable for all payments. It's a good way for those with thin or nonexistent credit to build up their credit.

If you have bad credit, focus on handling your debt better in the future. The best way to boost your credit score is to rectify past mistakes. And if you can't qualify for a traditional credit card or loan, consider signing up for credit builder loans. These are sometimes advertised as fresh start loans and can be used by those with poor credit (Konsko, 2020). With these loans, you make monthly payments, and your lender deposits these amounts into a savings account, allowing you to start building borrowing history. At the end of your term, you'll get access to the money in this savings account, minus any interest payments and fees. If you do opt for this, just make sure you can keep up with the monthly payments.

THE RIGHT WAY TO USE A CREDIT CARD

Credit cards can help you build good credit, provided you use them the right way. Here are the best tips for you to use them wisely:

- Pay your balance in full, every time. Why? Imagine buying a purse worth $1,000 and paying it in full. You won't pay a cent more than what it costs. If you paid it using a credit card at 20% interest and paid just the minimum payment instead, it would take you five years to pay it off and would cost you $1,486. You'll pay close to 50% more for the bag by doing this.

- If you don't have cash to buy something, don't buy it on a card.

- Never utilize more than 30% of your credit limit.

- Use cash back credit cards or cards that offer rewards. Use online tools to compare the best cards offered. Don't chase rewards, though. Be conscious of how you spend your money. Don't buy more just because you're receiving cash or rewards.

- Switch to a no-fee card or ask for the fees to be waived (Sethi, 2009). Also, try to negotiate a lower interest rate. Obviously, this doesn't always work, but it's worth a shot. If you don't ask, you don't get.

- Keep one or two card accounts active for a long time, and spend money on them using these tips. You'll build a lengthy credit history over time.

MANAGING AND REDUCING DEBT

If you're carrying significant levels of debt, you probably have a fair amount of tension in your neck and shoulders. Fun fact: I had to have a monthly masseuse budget to deal with the physical repercussions of debt stress. It's a thing.

Thankfully, I've listed a few steps below to help reduce your debt burden. But before we get into that, I need you to relax those shoulders, take a deep breath, and have some chocolate.

Step 1: Figure out who you owe money to and how much. Your credit report will list this. Or you can simply dig up your latest statements and log in to your student loan portal to figure this out. To track this information, I've created a simple spreadsheet you can find at www.30daymoneyschool.com.

Step 2: Choose a debt repayment method. Choosing the right method to repay your debt goes a long way toward eliminating it. There are two methods that work best: the debt snowball and the debt avalanche.

Let's look at the snowball method first. List all your debts in order of their outstanding balance, and pay the lowest one off in full while making minimum payments for the others.

Let's say you have a balance of $100 on a credit card and need to make minimum payments worth $500 on other debt. If you can devote $600 to eliminating debt, pay the $100 off in full and use the remaining $500 to pay monthly minimums. The following month, either pay off the lowest remaining debt in full or pay as much of its principal down while making minimum monthly payments on the remaining debt. Keep doing this until all your debt is repaid.

The debt avalanche method is mentally tougher to execute, but it works better. List all your debt on the basis of the interest rate you're being charged, irrespective of the balance. You'll now pay in full the debt that carries the highest interest rate, and you'll make minimum payments on the other debts. Keep doing this until you've eliminated all your debt.

Personally, I'm pro-Avalanche. It just makes a lot more sense. Take a look at the table below, for example. It shows how much interest you'd pay on your credit card debt vs. student loans over the course of 10 years (Young, 2020). Because credit card debt has a much higher interest rate, delaying repayment of that will cost you a lot more in the long-term.

Debt Type	Interest Rate (%)	Total Interest Paid ($)
Credit Card	16.97%	$4,915
Undergraduate Student Loan	4.53%	$743
Graduate Student Loan	6.08%	$1,005

Table 1: Interest on Credit Card Debt and Student Loans (Young, 2020)

Interest paid is based on $10,000 total for all loan types paid over a five-year term. Federal student loan rates are accurate for the 2019–2020 academic school year.

Both of these methods work well, but a lot depends on how you're psychologically built. If you receive a boost from looking at a shrinking list of debt, the snowball method works best. If you're a rational sort and can see that you'll pay your debt off much more quickly using the avalanche method, then adopt that. You can use the calculator at https://www.vertex42.com/Calculators/debt-reduction-calculator.html to figure out how quickly you can pay off your debt using either method.

Step 3: Work to reduce current debt loads. Here's how you can do this:

- Negotiate your interest rates – Call your credit card company and convince them to lower your APR (Annual Percentage Rate). This sounds more difficult than it is. In most cases, they're pretty desperate to keep you. So research what other credit card companies are offering and use that as leverage.
- Consider student loan refinancing and consolidation (covered later in the chapter).
- Refinance existing car loans or mortgages.

Step 4: Free up some money for debt repayment. There's a long list of saving hacks in the next chapter. Explore those options to help reduce your living expenses. If you can reduce your rent from $500 per month to $100 per month, that's $400 more in your pocket. Get a roommate or move in with your parents. It'll be worth it when you're debt-free.

Step 5: Beat that debt and be free! You can do this.

HOW TO HANDLE STUDENT LOANS

As promised, I will go into a bit more detail about our forever-favorite form of debt: student loans. Let's begin by looking at the student loan situation in the UK.

- Tuition is capped at GBP 9,000, and student loans are capped as well. Loan payments are capped at 9% of your income, and you need to pay only if your income is greater than GBP 25,725 per year (Base, 2020).
- If you cannot pay your loan back within 30 years or suffer a disability or death, it's written off.
- For our UK peeps, it's probably best to focus on paying down other debt first.

For those in the US, the picture is a bit more complex:

- There are no loan limits, and payments start six months after graduation. The debt is not written off.
- There are a few options to help you manage and reduce your student loan debt.
- If you have a steady job and good credit, consider

refinancing your loan. This basically means replacing your loan with a new one that has a lower interest rate.

- Alternatively, you can apply for student loan debt consolidation. This is a fancy term for bringing all your outstanding loans together to make just one payment every month (assuming you have more than one loan).
- In certain situations you can also apply for income-driven repayment plans or student loan forgiveness.

Let's look at these options in more detail.

Student Loan Forgiveness

Want to do some good in the world? Well, why not kill two birds with one stone and get your loan forgiven at the same time.

- Under the Public Service Loan Forgiveness Program, you may be eligible for loan forgiveness after 120 qualifying payments if you've worked full-time for an eligible employer within the public sector for the entirety of that period. Public sector means government or not-for-profit organizations.
- There is also a Teacher Loan Forgiveness program for teachers who work in specific schools with children from low-income families.
- Check out the Federal Student Aid website (https://studentaid.gov/manage-loans/forgiveness-

cancellation/public-service) for more details on how this works.

Federal Loan Consolidation

A federal loan is essentially a government loan. Here are the pros and cons of consolidating federal student loans.

Pros:

- Simplified loan repayment process – just one loan and one bill to deal with
- Lower monthly payments since the repayment term is usually much longer (anything from 12–30 years)
- Fixed interest rates that won't change over the course of your loan period
- Your consolidated loan is seen as a new loan. That means if you've used up your unemployment and economic hardship benefits, you'll be eligible to apply for them again.

Cons:

- You won't receive lower interest rates.
- You might end up paying more overall, even if your monthly payments are lower since the term of your loan is longer. This is because longer-term loans result in paying more interest.

- You will lose your grace period if you happen to be in it currently. That's the six-month window you get before having to start repaying your student loans.
- Any special borrower benefits you received from your previous loan will be lost.
- If you were making payments toward student loan forgiveness or an income-driven repayment plan, none of those payments count once you consolidate. It's a new loan, so you'll need to start again.
- You can only consolidate once. If interest rates take a dip after you consolidate, tough luck! You're stuck with the rate you originally agreed to.

Private Loan Consolidation

Private loans are not managed by the government but by private organizations. Consolidation conditions vary according to the institutions, so make sure you check with them first.

Pros:

- Simplified loan repayment process – just one loan and one bill to deal with
- Interest rates are based on market conditions and your credit score, which means you might be offered a lower rate than when you initially applied. This is especially true if you have started working and built up your credit.

Cons:

- If you have bad credit, you may not get a favorable interest rate.
- Unlike federal loan consolidation, your debt might carry a variable interest rate. That means your monthly payment might fluctuate over time.

Income-Driven Repayment Plans

Income-driven repayment plans can cut student loan repayments to 10%–15% of your discretionary income (Federal Student Aid, 2020). You can apply at studentloans.gov. If your income is low and loan balances are large, this is your best option.

There are four options the U.S. government offers (*Federal Student Aid*, 2020):

- ***Revised Pay As You Earn Repayment (REPAYE) plan*** – This usually amounts to 10% of your discretionary income.
- ***Pay As You Earn (PAYE) plan*** – This is also 10% of your income, but the payment won't exceed the amount as determined by the standard 10-year repayment plan.
- ***Income-Based Repayment (IBR) plan*** – For those who borrowed before July 2014, this is limited to 10%

of your discretionary income. If you borrowed after that, it's capped at 15% of your discretionary income.

- *Income-Contingent Repayment (ICR) plan* – This is capped at 20% of your discretionary income or the amount you would pay on a standard 12-year repayment plan, whichever is less.

The repayment period ranges from 20–25 years for all plans. If you have an outstanding balance at the end of that period, your loans are forgiven. There are different eligibility requirements that keep changing, so it's best to check the federal student aid site for updates.

Refinancing Your Student Loans

- Refinancing means replacing your existing federal or private loans with a new private student loan that has a lower interest rate. Lower interest rates are the primary reason people choose to refinance.
- Refinancing can also lower your monthly payments by allowing you to extend your repayment term, should you choose to do so.
- It allows you to remove any co-signers and assume full ownership of your loans.
- It disqualifies you from federal assistance and forgiveness programs.

Next Steps: Consolidate or Refinance?

- Consolidation is the better option if:
- You are juggling multiple federal loans and finding them hard to manage. Consolidation will simplify this and reduce your risk of default.
- You wish to take advantage of federal protection, assistance, and benefit programs.
- Refinancing is the better option if:
- You don't care about or don't qualify for federal benefits.
- Your main goal is to lower your interest rate and save money.
- You want to change the owner of the loan.

Pro Tips: Wipe Out That Student Loan

- Automate your payments. Lenders offer you a discount of around 0.25% when you opt to do this.
- Apply excess payments to reduce principal. Use the calculator at https://www.credible.com/blog/calculators/student-loan-repayment-calculator/ to estimate payoff schedules if you reduce principal.
- Check if your employer offers student loan assistance programs.
- If you receive a windfall, allocate that money to pay down your loan principal.

- Tackle it one bit at a time. It can be overwhelming, but aim for consistency. That is what produces results.

ACTION PLAN – DAYS 13–15

If you have zero debt:

- Apply for a credit card and start charging a small amount on it. Pay your balance off immediately.
- If applying for a regular credit card is not possible, consider some of the other options outlined above to start building your credit.

If you have debt:

- Make a list of all of your debts—who you owe and how much. Feel free to use my debt tracking spreadsheet at www.30daymoneyschool.com.
- Decide on a debt repayment method.
- Consider options to help reduce your debt load (e.g., student loan consolidation vs. refinancing).
- Free up some cash for debt repayment.
- Start making payments.
- If you're still in college, make student loan payments with all the spare change you have. You'll save on interest in the long run.
- Make sure you update your budget tracker with your

debt repayment allocations under the Forecast tab. Also make sure you are updating your actuals on a monthly basis.

- If things get overwhelming, remember this quote:

"It does not matter how slowly you go as long as you do not stop."

— CONFUCIUS

7

KEEP (MOST OF) YOUR MONEY TO YOURSELF – SPENDING & SAVING HACKS

"He who buys what he does not need, steals from himself."

— SWEDISH PROVERB

What do you spend your money on? I'd be real concerned if you don't know the answer to that by now, particularly after conducting my super fun and thorough personal spending analysis! Well, my reasons for asking are twofold: (1) I'm nosy, and (2) I'm concerned about the United States. Did you know that Americans spend more than $18,000 per year on eating out, subscription, and drinks with friends (Holmes, 2019)? That's $1,500 per month on outside food, booze, and Netflix. Talk about #FirstWorldProblems. I'm not saying we don't need these things in our lives, but do they matter enough to warrant this much expenditure?

Think about it this way. A fancy cocktail costs you $15, and you have two of those every Friday night for a whole year. That's $1,560 a year and $31,200 over a 20-year period. See how little choices add up to poor long-term decisions? Imagine what else you could do with that money. Let's assume you earn $15 an hour. Those cocktails aren't just costing you $15; they're costing you 104 hours of your life each year.

Saving is hard. We are saddled with debt and high costs of living. Then there's the global pandemic and all its repercussions on the economy. And that is why I encourage you to question your spending choices. That fancy cocktail might make you feel good now, but 20 years down the road, you may regret that choice. Limit yourself to two fancy drinks per month, and you've saved more than $21,000. Insane, right?

In this chapter, I'll be touching on the psychology of spending and how understanding that can help curb impulsive spending decisions. I'll also be giving you some top tips to reduce expenses and save more of those $dolla.

THE PSYCHOLOGY OF SPENDING

"Don't be a sheep!" screams the overly passionate motivational speaker as the audience shares baffled glances. We often behave like sheep without realizing it. You see, sheep travel in herds, mindlessly following each other. As humans, we also tend to follow the crowd. Whether it's fashion, career choices, or simply the way we speak, what others around us are doing influences the decisions we make for ourselves. It's adorable when sheep do it. Humans, not so much.

Think about something as simple as your decision to buy this book. I know some of you just love me for who I am, and I appreciate that. But the majority of those who choose to buy this book will do so because others have said it's good. They'll read the reviews, see how high it's ranking on Amazon, or ask friends and family. Nothing wrong with that. I would do the same. But the point I'm making is that we have an innate tendency to do what others are doing. In social psychology, that is called herd mentality. In layman's terms, it's peer pressure. And it can significantly influence our spending patterns.

We're bombarded with images on social media of unrealistic lifestyle standards. You see pictures of people posing next to fancy cars and making it rain in clubs. Your first instinct is to want a piece of that life. That is normal. Everyone wants a good life. However, if you don't curb yourself, you're going to end up doing a ton of harm to your financial life, not to mention your self-esteem.

Heard of FOMO? For the benefit of our more sophisticated readers, FOMO stands for fear of missing out. As sad as its sounds, FOMO usually occurs when we closely follow the activity of others on social media and feel they are leading better, more exciting lives than we are. Something as small as your friends going to a new restaurant without you can trigger FOMO. A YouTube celebrity buying a private island in the Caribbean can also put a slight downer on things. According to Charles Schwab, FOMO is actually fueling American spending. Schwab's 2019 Modern Wealth Index Survey shows that more than a third of Americans confess to spending more than they can afford because of images and experiences shared on social media ("FOMO Fuels American Spending"). Now, don't freak out on me. I'm not telling you to delete all your social media accounts. I'm saying to take everything you see with a grain of salt. You don't know how your friends or those bloggers are paying for things or how much debt they might be in. More importantly, don't compare yourself to others. Let them live their life, and you live yours. They'll be the ones chasing you down when you've got that million-dollar mansion in 30 years.

Prioritize the Long Term over the Short Term

Have you ever heard of the marshmallow test? It was a study conducted in the 1960s by child psychologist Walter Mischel (2015). Mischel's objective was to measure self-control in children. He devised a simple experiment.

He sat a bunch of five-year-old kids down in front of a marshmallow (or candy) and told them that if they could resist eating it for 15 minutes, they'd receive another. Some kids ate the marshmallow while others literally sat on their hands to earn the higher reward. Mischel published his findings and went about his way.

Fifteen years later, Mischel randomly decided to revisit his old experiments and looked up his former subjects. He wasn't expecting to find anything, but find something he did. It turned out that all the kids who resisted temptation and prioritized long-term gains over short-term ones uniformly scored higher on tests, were in more prestigious universities, and had generally done better in life compared to the ones who opted to eat the marshmallow that was placed in front of them.

The lesson here is simple: Prioritizing long-term benefits over short-term ones is the route to prosperity. No more FOMO. Be a trend-setter, not a follower.

Rewire Your Brain to Spend Less

1. Make a list of the triggers that cause you to spend more than you planned. For example, have you noticed that you spend more on groceries when you shop while hungry? Or do you spend on retail therapy when you've had a bad day? This was something I was particularly bad at. I would buy shoes to make myself feel better (so stupid, I know now). When I started to separate my money into savings accounts and most of it wasn't immediately accessible to me, it made it much harder to do this.

2. Pay with cash. This is super helpful for the shopaholics and over-spenders out there. When I started on my personal finance journey, I realized it was much harder to part with physical cash than it was to spend on a card where I couldn't immediately see the money being taken away from me and draining my account balance. As my wallet emptied, guilt and fear kicked in. This helped me be disciplined. Remember, personal finance is 90% behavioral and only 10% math. If you can work out what triggers certain negative behaviors and use the techniques in this book to tackle them, you'll be just fine.

3. Be curious and learn. Educate yourself on all things money. This book is an excellent first step, but don't stop here. Keep reading, and keep asking questions. I have a Facebook group set up where you can ask me or the other members anything you like. It's called 30-Day Money School: How to Budget, Save & Invest for Beginners. Join us, and join other groups, too.

If you have specific questions to ask, feel free to book in a free 15 minute coaching call with me: https://calendly.com/30daymoneyschool/15min

4. Have a positive money mindset. Everyone has some unconscious beliefs about money, and that influences how we act and manage our money. As discussed above, a lot of us see money as a means to fit in rather than a tool to create happy and successful lives for ourselves. Personally, I grew up being taught that money was there to be spent, that worrying too much about saving and not spending was a stingy attitude. "Your money won't go with you to your grave," I heard often. While I completely agree with not making money a central part of your life, it's important to use it wisely if you have a vision of a certain kind of life for yourself, one that doesn't involve working 60 plus hours a week until you're 60 years old. Surround yourself with people who have similar goals. Make sure you're part of a community that will support you and hold you accountable. You'll achieve your goals much faster that way.

5. Focus on creating long-lasting change instead of applying short-term band-aids.

Become Money-Conscious

In order to curb your spending, it's important for you to start thinking in terms of value as opposed to price. For example, a $2,000 computer is expensive compared to a $700 computer. But if the expensive one lasts nearly a decade while the cheaper one needs to be replaced after two years, then the value the expensive computer delivers is tremendous. Value versus price is at the heart of being money-conscious.

Before every potential expense, ask yourself if the price you're paying is worth the value you'll receive. For example, if you love hanging out with your friends and going out, is it necessary for you to spend excessive amounts of money on overpriced drinks? Is it possible for you to derive similar levels of pleasure by having a few drinks at home first and then paying for just one expensive drink later, or choosing just a (shock and horror) cup of coffee? These questions might seem absurd at first, but they encourage you to examine all your spending choices.

Distill experiences down to their essence. What are you really spending your money on, and what is it that truly gives you pleasure? Look at every potential purchase as a bowl of ice cream. You could buy a single scoop or you could buy an entire sundae loaded with goodies. Can a single scoop give you the same value as a full sundae? Your favorite part is the ice cream itself. You're not big on the extras. All you really need is something to satisfy your sweet tooth after dinner. So do you have to buy a sundae every time? Probably not. Eating it once in a while is a nice treat, but you certainly don't have to spend that much money all the time. Examine your purchasing choices like this. It takes work, but your wallet will thank you for it.

Always return to your budget and evaluate whether you have the cash to afford a particular expense. Avoid the temptation of increasing your expenses as your income increases. This is called lifestyle creep, and it can hurt your savings. I'm not saying you need to live in a tiny apartment and share toilets for the rest of your life. It's just that your expenses should increase at a far slower rate than your income does.

Consider making changes to your lifestyle that can deliver similar benefits but reduce expenses. For example, working out at a park or at home can eliminate gym membership fees. You can buy a bunch of gym equipment for a one-off payment of $100 and never have to spend a penny again. Be creative. Join online communities about fitness to keep you motivated, and follow fitness junkies who often host free online workouts. When there is a will, there is always a way!

Cooking at home saved me $100 per month, which equates to $1,200 per year. All these little savings do eventually add up to a significant amount. I'm not asking you to cut every expense. Instead, take a deep breath. Think before you spend. Your financial goals are everything. Is this going to hinder your long-term success?

MONEY-SAVING HACKS

Saving the money you need with the least sacrifice is all about being savvy and creative. It takes a bit of work, but the tips below will get you going. Just two to three small changes can save you hundreds if not thousands each year.

1. The best thing you can do for your wallet is to start using a cash-back rewards app or other money-saving apps. These apps alert you to coupons you can use when shopping for groceries and other essentials. Honey is one such great app you can install and use for free. You can download it at https://www.join-honey.com.

2. Stop shopping at convenience stores and plan your grocery purchases ahead of time. The goods in these stores are marked up to high levels, and you can buy them for lower prices at supermarkets and other wholesale stores. They bank on being conveniently located—hence the name—but they are more expensive for providing that convenience. Make a shopping list before you buy groceries. This will help you avoid having to reach for random things. If you plan your grocery shopping well, you'll also have time to research coupons available. Don't worry about looking like a miser—it's your money after all! Even Warren Buffett and Bill Gates use coupons when they eat at McDonald's. If that's what it takes to join the billionaire's club, then I say it's worth it!

3. Many supermarkets sell their own brand of goods. They are usually of comparable quality to brand items but much cheaper. Buy these as much as possible. For example, cleaning supplies and other intermittent purchases don't need to be fancy. Choose generic brands, and you'll save a lot of money. Another idea is to buy as much as possible in bulk from a big box store, assuming you have the cash for it. For example, essentials such as toiletries and toothpaste can be bought in bulk. You can buy food in bulk as well, but be careful with perishable items.

4. Buy used items as much as possible. Cars are an obvious choice. Used clothes might not sound appealing to you, but thrift stores have real bargains these days. You can wear high fashion clothes for bargain-bin prices.

5. Cooking at home will do more to save you money than anything else. Prep your meals twice a week and learn how to cook. It's a lot simpler than you think. Simply throw your food into the oven and wait for it to cook. You can prepare meals in bulk and store them for reheating later in the week. Save eating out for the weekends or special occasions. You'll value it more.

6. DIY (do it yourself) on any repairs you can confidently tackle instead of paying someone else. That broken door knob doesn't need to cost you $50. A combination of YouTube, tips from Dad, and persistence will get it fixed in no time. I promise.

7. Share expenses with your friends as much as possible when you go out. Have a potluck dinner instead of the usual drinks at the bar. All of you will save some money. Meet that casual acquaintance at a Starbucks instead of buying them a round at the bar. Carpool with friends or others as much as possible. You can find carpools online as well as a ton of free stuff such as furniture.

8. Review your subscriptions and cancel the ones you rarely use. Unsubscribe from e-mails for online shopping services. These have tempting offers that are designed to get you to click on things you don't need. Delete your card information from shopping portals and disable one-click purchases.

9. Utilities can cost you a significant sum if you're not careful. Check the insulation in your home or apartment and invest in this to reduce your bills. If you happen to live in an area where it gets really cold, insulation will save you tons of money per month. Opt for energy-saving appliances. They cost more up front, but they'll save you money in the long run. Some utility providers can give you budget heating plans that will lower your expenses throughout the year, so inquire about these as well.

10. Bundling is your friend when it comes to utilities such as a phone plan, the Internet, and streaming subscriptions. Cable operators these days force you to sign up for Internet plus cable even if you plan on using streaming services. See if you can opt for an Internet-only plan. Alternatively, opt for a high data mobile Internet plan and use it to stream services on your TV. Consider whether you even need streaming. You can find entertainment online for free without the need to pirate or steal content. Are you willing to give up your Netflix shows? Stay away from them for a month, and you'll notice that you don't miss them.

11. Opt for phone plans that give you a free phone, and don't purchase plans that give you "free" iPhones or some fancy gadget that comes with a monthly payment. Sign up for plans that give you rebates or free devices. Always shop around for the lowest prices.

12. Whenever you're in the market for a product or service, compare prices. Many people don't compare prices and reach for the first option. Instead, speak to multiple service providers and do your research online to find the lowest prices. Many retailers offer price-matching services but don't always advertise them. If you can find a similar item for a lower price online, ask them if you can have it at that price. Always check online to see if there's someone who can provide utilities for lower prices. If this is the case, check with your landlord to see if they're okay with you switching providers.

13. Likewise, insurance companies often draw you in with a cheap introductory first-year price and then start hiking the price from the second year onward. Always shop around for car insurance and medical plans. Health insurance is a world of its own in the US, and it takes some time to learn how it works. I'll deal with this in great detail in Chapter 8 on insurance. Shop around for the best rates, and make sure you purchase a dental plan as well since that is not part of a regular health insurance plan.

14. There are lots of great websites out there for comparing utility bills and insurance policy prices, and they're incredibly easy to use. So please do your research.

15. If you're sharing housing expenses with someone, consider using an app such as Splitwise or Splitoo to track who's been paying on time.

Special Tips for College Students

If you're in college, you're broke and you know it. However, that doesn't mean you can't save money.

1. Free pizza? Hell yeah! Every college campus has free events and concerts. Use these as much as possible. Certain events and festivals have free food, so make sure to attend those. I gained a few pounds in college thanks to free pizza three times a week.

2. Student ID cards can get you discounts almost everywhere, so make sure you use them. Public transportation, restaurants, and movie theaters are just some of the places that offer these discounts. Having said that, remember that just because you get things cheaper doesn't mean you should buy more. In college, I ended up spending most of my allowance on clothes I didn't really like and definitely didn't need, just because I could. Don't be like me.

3. Use the library to rent textbooks as much as possible instead of buying them new. If you need your own copy, buy used textbooks. A top tip is to buy international versions of textbooks instead of the ones printed in the US or the UK. These books will have lower quality paper but will be a lot cheaper. They'll contain the same information, though, so it's not as if you'll miss out on anything.

4. Evaluate whether living in dorms is cheaper or more expensive than off-campus housing. This will really depend on where your college is. Look at listings in your area and compare the costs of living in an apartment with roommates versus living in the dorms. Also, don't forget to check if your tuition assistance and financial aid covers off-campus housing.

5. College meal plans can also vary depending on your area. Some college meal plans are a lot cheaper than food at restaurants, but on some campuses, they're more expensive. Whatever the case is, they'll be more expensive than cooking at home. Consider getting a job at one of the student cafeterias. You'll be able to receive a meal for your shift, which will reduce your expenses.

6. Another great way to have your living costs subsidized is to become a resident advisor (RA). You can live in the dorms for free, and other living costs such as meals might be subsidized as well. You'll have to deal with administrative tasks, but given how much money you'll save, it's worth it.

Negotiating Large Purchases

The two largest purchases you'll make are a home and a car. A home is a massive purchase that you'll pay for at least 20–30 years. Most people opt for 30-year mortgages, so any cost-saving you can capture up front makes a huge difference. Before visiting a property, check to see how long it's been on the market. The longer it's been for sale, the more leverage you have, no matter how stubborn the seller may seem.

When you inspect the property, you can request the seller to make certain changes. As long as they are cosmetic, the seller will probably agree to it. It's also a good idea to apply for mortgage pre-approval and present the seller with this letter as proof that you're serious. This guarantees a faster sale, and the seller may be more willing to lower the price.

Remember closing costs? Well, you can reduce that expense as well by asking the seller to pay a portion of them. Ask your agent to prepare accurate comps. A comp is a report that compares selling prices of similar properties. Check websites such as Zillow and Roofstock to figure out possible sales prices.

When it comes to buying a car, you should use all your bargaining skills. Car salespeople have a variety of tricks up their sleeves. The first trick is to get you to focus on the monthly payment you want to make. That is referred to as the four-square method, and it is a trap. Focus on the sticker price first, and then negotiate hard. Show them listings online of cheaper prices and push them to lower the price.

Try not to arrive at a sales lot in a taxi. The sales guys will think you're desperate and more likely to drive one of their cars off the lot. Arrive in your own vehicle, conduct thorough research online, and don't be afraid to visit the lot a few times to negotiate the price.

A good tip is to buy a rental fleet car or an older police car. These cars are usually well maintained, and you can get them dirt cheap. You can check online for dealers who stock these cars. Car auctions offer great bargains as well.

Use services such as CARFAX to run the VINs of prospective cars to figure out where they've been and what their history is. All this gives you a lot of leverage over the dealer. Above all, remember to buy a used car and pay as much of a down payment as possible, assuming you can't pay for it in full.

ACTION PLAN – DAYS 16–18

- Pick up the phone and start negotiating your bills.
- Pick five other things you can do right now, based on the tips in this chapter, to reduce your expenses.
- Start practicing money-consciousness. If emotional spending is a problem for you, list your spending triggers and ask friends or family to hold you accountable. Put reminders on your phone or your bedroom wall so you don't do anything crazy in the moment.

"The quickest way to double your money is to fold it in half and put it in your back pocket."

— WILL ROGERS

8

PREPARING FOR THE UNEXPECTED – INSURANCE MATTERS

"Buying insurance cannot change your life but it prevents your life from being changed....You will not turn bankrupt because of buying insurance but you will cause your loved ones to turn bankrupt if you don't."

— JACK MA

That's a lot of words from Jack Ma. However, as the founder of Alibaba, I say we hear him out. You might be thinking, *Insurance is for old people. I'm as fit as a fiddle! Isn't it just another needless expense?* Not quite. There are many types of insurance. In the US in particular, health insurance is a must. If you have a catastrophic illness and don't have insurance, you're pretty much guaranteed to go bankrupt. We've talked a lot in this book about planning for the future and prioritizing the long term over the short. Insurance is a critical part of that planning process. Health insurance, car insurance, life insurance, and disability insurance are all there to protect you and your loved ones in the event that things go wrong.

In 2018, 27.5 million Americans had no health insurance (Berchick, Barnett, & Upton, 2019). In 2019, 57% of Americans had life insurance, but 70% of them were underinsured (McKay, 2020). Clearly, insurance is not on every American's priority list (although some simply can't afford it). And clearly, we don't really understand it either.

All forms of insurance work pretty much the same. You pay a premium every month and receive protection for a specified dollar amount for a specified number of situations, depending on the type of insurance and level of coverage. As bored as you may be right now, I'm going to give you an overview of the most important types of insurance and how they work. Then I'll give you some nice, easy homework at the end. You know how I roll.

LIFE INSURANCE

Breaking news: We're all gonna die! Some earlier than others. Some with partners and dependents. Sorry, I don't mean to sound morbid. I just don't think you'd take me seriously otherwise. Life insurance can prevent your family from falling into financial ruin after you're gone. These policies pay a certain amount to your loved ones (your beneficiaries) after your death. The amount will help them pay for your funeral as well as regular expenses that still come due. Broadly speaking, there are two kinds of life insurance: term and whole.

Let's look at term life insurance. This type of policy only covers you for a fixed period of time and is unfortunately only worth the investment if you pass away during the specified term. If you pass before the policy expires, your beneficiaries will receive a payout. If the term expires before your death, they get nothing. You sometimes have to answer questions about your health or get a medical examination in order to qualify for a term life insurance policy. If you renew the policy after it expires, the premium usually increases because you are now older. The upshot is that the premiums are really low for the kind of coverage benefit you receive.

Whole life policies, also called permanent insurance, are more expensive, but they'll last forever (as long as you keep paying the premiums, of course). And your premium amount is fixed, so it won't increase over time. Whole life policies also have an investment component known as cash value, which means you can accumulate interest on part of your payment. If you're ever in need of funds, the company will lend you that amount in the form of a loan. Just remember that unless you pay back that loan before you pass, the company will deduct the amount you borrowed from the final payout to your beneficiaries.

A much better option is to opt for term life insurance and use the difference between the premium you pay for term insurance and what you would pay for permanent insurance for an investment opportunity with a better rate of return (e.g., a low-cost index fund with an 8%–10% average annual rate of return). It's a much better bang for your buck!

If you adopt and implement the principles taught in this book, you don't need a whole life (permanent) insurance policy. You'll have more than enough money saved up and invested to self-insure.

Who Needs Life Insurance?

Not everyone needs life insurance. You probably don't need it if:

- You are single with no dependents.
- You have a partner who doesn't rely on your income.
- You have a partner and/or family but no outstanding debts, and there are other assets that can be liquidated upon your death.

However, if the conditions below apply to you, buying a policy is prudent (Light, 2018):

- You have young children who are dependent on you financially. Life insurance is necessary to protect their future.
- You're married and very much dependent on two incomes. For your spouse to continue living the same sort of lifestyle after you pass, life insurance is important.
- You're a business owner with business partners and/or many employees. Insurance will help ensure business continuity in the event of your death.
- You own a large estate that cannot easily be liquidated. You'll likely need insurance to cover the cost of inheritance taxes.

Think about how much coverage you need and how long you need to be covered. The amount of the policy should be in line with the kind of life you want your loved ones to lead after your death. Remember, it isn't just current costs that need to be covered; future costs have to be covered as well. Always compare quotes from different insurers. Your employer may also offer you a life insurance policy at a discounted rate.

DISABILITY INSURANCE

Disability insurance is a form of insurance that's often ignored or misunderstood. Disability is one of the most common causes of bankruptcy. Disability insurance is most necessary for those whose jobs require manual labor, although it can make sense for other professions as well. Some of the most common disability insurance claims relate to cancer, musculoskeletal disorders, and depression.

The Social Security Administration estimates that more than 25% of 20-year-olds are likely to suffer from some form of disability by the time they reach the age of 67 ("Fact Sheet," 2020). If you're completely reliant on your income and if your savings are next to non-existent, then disability insurance is a no-brainer. Get yourself a quote, and then check your budget to see if you can afford it. If you can't afford it now, what do you have to do to be able to afford it?

There are two types of disability insurance: short-term and long-term. Short-term disability insurance coverage begins immediately but only covers you for a short period of time, usually a few months. The typical term is six months. Long-term disability coverage has a six-month waiting period where it doesn't pay anything, and then it covers the insured person for either a set period of time (anything between 2-10 years), or until retirement (age 65).

Ideally, if you suffer from a disability at work, your emergency savings should cover your living expenses for the initial six-month period before insurance kicks in. So long-term coverage is the better option. If you work at a high-risk job, then your employer should offer you disability insurance as a standard benefit. Get in touch with an insurance professional if your employer doesn't offer such a plan.

Your premiums will depend on your existing health and the nature of your job. Make sure you shop around as much as possible to determine the lowest rates available.

HEALTH INSURANCE

Let's get the easy stuff out of the way first. If you're in the UK, you're entitled to receive free healthcare from the National Health Service (NHS) throughout your life. While you may sometimes face lengthy wait times, the quality of care is high, and the most serious concerns will be a priority. If you wish, you can opt for private health insurance, which gives you access to more treatments than offered by the NHS. Check with your employer if this is offered as part of your employment benefits.

In the US, things are a bit more complicated (as always). Health insurance pays for a portion of your treatments when you are injured or become sick. Health insurance has become a political football that both political parties toss around and hoodwink the public into thinking they're doing something about. The reality is that insurance in America is a huge industry, and nothing is likely change anytime soon. That makes it essential for you to learn how health insurance works.

Health insurance was probably your first true introduction to the adult world. You were covered by your parents' health insurance plan and then by your college's insurance plan. One day you graduated and realized you're on your own. No time to shop for shoes anymore. Time to start shopping for health plans!

Having said that, you can actually remain on your parents' health insurance plan until the age of 26 (McCarthy, 2020). Even if you're married and not living with them, Mom and Dad can have your back until then (should they choose to do so; you'd better behave). But let's talk about what to do after that.

Choosing a policy is of paramount importance because it determines how much money you pay each month. It's tempting to choose policies with a low monthly payment, but that might not offer you adequate coverage.

Briefly, here are the terms you need to understand in order to find the best deal possible:

- *Deductible* – This is the portion of a medical bill that you have to pay.

- *Co-Payment (Copay)* – This is a flat fee you must pay for each medical service you receive. The amount is considered part of your deductible.
- *Network* – Your plan pays more at certain medical facilities (your network). You can usually receive medical care at other facilities (out-of-network clinics or hospitals), but the policy won't pay as much of your bill.
- *Inpatient/Outpatient* – If you're formally admitted to a hospital, you're an inpatient. An emergency room or clinic visit is considered outpatient. Deductibles and co-pays will differ depending on whether you're an inpatient or outpatient. Coverage will also vary if the medical facility is in network or out-of-network.
- *Out-of-pocket limit* – This is the maximum amount of money you'll pay in one year for treatment.

High-deductible plans usually have lower monthly payments. Check the combination of monthly payment, deductible, and co-pay to figure out what makes the most sense. Remember that the out-of-pocket amount you'll pay includes your deductible and co-pay. It's also important to note that health insurance companies in the US are not allowed to deny coverage or charge you more if you have a pre-existing condition.

The best way to choose the right policy is to ask yourself the following questions:

- How good or bad is my health? How often do I need to visit a doctor? If you have to go often, it's better to opt for a plan with a low deductible and co-pay. Your premiums will be higher, but your out-of-pocket costs will be lower.

- If you don't go to the doctor very often, choose a high-deductible plan. Your monthly premiums will be lower.

- What are my current health insurance options? Employers often offer health insurance as part of your job perks or benefits. If your employer's plan doesn't meet all your medical needs, consider getting an additional health insurance plan.

You should also have dental insurance. A lot of us ignore that and regret it when our poor teeth start rotting due to a lack of care. Dental plans are inexpensive, so don't neglect them. Your teeth will thank you.

CAR INSURANCE

These days, pretty much every state requires you to purchase insurance within a certain period after you drive a vehicle off the lot. Car insurance covers not just damages to your vehicle but also damages you cause to someone else's vehicle. If that sounds like mumbo jumbo, don't worry, I'll break it down.

States that require insurance have minimum coverage requirements. Google can tell you what those are. Briefly, here are
some of the basic things auto insurance covers:

- *Liability* – pays for costs related to another person's
  injuries or damage to their property
- *Collision* – pays to repair your damaged vehicle or
  pays the value of your car if the cost to fix it is more
  than it's worth
- *Uninsured motorist* – covers you if the driver you're
  in an accident with is uninsured
- *Comprehensive* – covers damages from things such as
  theft, vandalism, fire, or natural damages
- *Personal injury* – covers medical expenses for you
  and other passengers as a result of an accident

Depending on the level of coverage you opt for, insurance can
pay for damages to your car if you drive it into a tree (*been
there, done that*). If you bump into someone else's car while
parking (again, guilty as charged!), insurance may also pay for
damage to the other car. In the event your car gets stolen,
broken into, or totaled, insurance can help cover those damages.
Like health insurance, there is a deductible and an out-of-
pocket limit. Usually, you can use the autobody shop of your
choice to fix your car. Note that insurance doesn't cover regular
maintenance on your car. You'll be responsible for that.

If you choose to have a high deductible for your car insurance plan, you'll pay less per month for coverage. Low deductible plans will cost more per month, but you will pay less for each accident or incident.

Sadly, your car insurance premiums largely depend on your age, and there's not much you can do about that. The type of car you have also factors into your insurance premium. If you're a 22-year-old man driving a yellow V8 muscle car, you're pretty much checking all the boxes that classify you as high risk. It's a good idea to remain on your parents' policy for as long as possible, but you have to live at their address and the title to the car must be in their names. Check with their insurance company to see if that's possible and for how long you can do that.

Opting for boring vehicles with a ton of safety features reduces your premium. A good option for you to look into is bundling your car insurance with your renter's insurance or homeowner's insurance (I'll explain these shortly).

One final bit of wisdom is to keep a clean driving record, kids! Oh, and always shop around before choosing a policy.

RENTER'S AND HOMEOWNER'S INSURANCE

Did you know you're just as likely to be robbed if you're a renter as you are if you own your home? Okay, I don't actually have any statistics to back that up, but I'm trying to make a point here. Renter's insurance is just as important as homeowner's insurance, but many of us overlook that. If your place becomes uninhabitable (either due to an unscrupulous landlord or a fire, flood, or other natural disaster), then your landlord's homeowner's insurance will not cover your losses. It only covers theirs. Your renter's insurance can put you up in a hotel while your landlord fixes your place. If you happen to lose your possessions due to theft or damage, your renter's insurance can help you buy new things to replace those items. Your insurance company will pay you the approximate value of your possessions.

If you purchase a home and take out a mortgage, your lender will require you to have homeowner's insurance. This pays for damages to your home from natural disasters and pays the medical bills for all accidents that happen due to your negligence. For example, if Aunt Connie pays an unexpected visit and "accidentally" (*wink wink*) trips on a wire, falls down the stairs, or injures herself in any way on your property, you're legally liable for her medical bills. It was negligent of you to leave that wire there. Homeowner's insurance will cover her bills. It will also pay for damages to your property caused by fire, floods, storm damage, and more.

ACTION PLAN – DAYS 19–21

- Check to see if your employer has any insurance

benefits to offer you, including health insurance, dental insurance, life insurance, and disability insurance.

- List the types of insurance you need.
- Shop for the best plans and figure out the right deductibles and monthly payments you can make. Add these to your budget if you haven't done so previously.

9

THE UNAVOIDABLE OBLIGATION –
LET'S TALK TAXES

---

*"Today, it takes more brains and effort to make out
the income-tax form than it does to make the income."*

— ALFRED E. NEWMAN

W hat's the most terrifying entity in the world? Is it some terrorist organization? Is it the CIA? What about the secret police forces of authoritarian regimes around the world? Surely, Kim Jong-un's hairdressing team makes the list. While these organizations make the top 10, the number-one spot is occupied and will always be occupied by the Internal Revenue Service (IRS). If you're in the UK, it's Her Majesty's Revenue and Customs (HMRC) for you. Unless you're a US citizen, in which case you'll need to deal with both HMRC and the IRS (*Jeez*, good luck). These are the government agencies that oversee tax collection and enforce the tax laws.

Did you know that governments allocate more money to their tax investigation departments than they do to municipal law enforcement bodies or education (Friday, 2019)? And did you know that nine out of 10 Americans believe the tax code is far too complicated (Kurtzleben, 2017)? So as much as I hate talking about taxes, I felt it would be beneficial to give you an overview since no one else seems to be doing that. I would like to add a caveat, though, that it's always best to seek professional help from an accountant or tax advisor, particularly if your taxes are complex. But you also don't want to look like an absolute fool sitting in your accountant's office asking questions like "What is the IRS?"

Don't worry. I've got your back. I'll help you get this tax thing all figured out. First and foremost, you need to understand these three tax pillars:

- Ordinary income tax
- Capital gains tax
- Deductions and credits

Ordinary income refers to the income you earn throughout the year. Capital gains refers to the profits you make by selling investments. For example, if you buy a property for $100,000 and sell it for $200,000, you've made a capital gain of $100,000 (the difference between the sale price and the purchase price). Deductions and credits are items you can list on your tax return that lower your tax bill.

The initial part of this chapter deals with the American tax system, specifically Federal Income Taxes. The majority of US states also have some form of state taxation. State income tax rates and how they are applied can differ considerably from one state to the next. The state taxation laws of all fifty states are beyond the scope of this book, but hopefully the basics I cover in here will set you up well for that first meeting with your accountant or tax advisor! I'll address the UK tax system later in the chapter. The principles regarding the three pillars remain largely the same in either case (although deductions and credits are much more relevant in the US than the UK).

The second most important thing to understand is which forms to fill out. The IRS *loves* to make things complicated, so there are a bunch of forms out there. But that's what I'm here for, to simplify things for you. This is by no means an exhaustive list, so please always do your own research, particularly if you are self-employed or own a business. This mini glossary highlights the top four forms you need to be aware of for the purposes of this basic tax overview.

Form Name	What It's For
Form W-4	You don't file this or send it to the IRS. If you are employed, complete this form and give it to your employer. It tells your employer your tax filing status and how many dependents you can claim. You can also tell your employer to send the IRS extra money from your paycheck. The amount your employer withholds from your paycheck will be calculated according to your tax status and dependents and any extra money you have instructed them to withhold.
Form W-2	Your employer will give you Form W-2 after the end of the year. This form tells you how much you earned for the year and how much tax they withheld from your paycheck. A copy of this form goes to the IRS.
Form 1040	The form most US taxpayers submit to the IRS. It summarizes your income, dependents, adjustments, deductions, and credits for the tax year in question. I'll cover each of these elements later on.
Form 1099	Anyone who has paid you money in any capacity other than formal employment, will give you a Form 1099. For example any interest, dividends or capital gains will be provided on a 1099-INT, 1099-DIV, or 1099-B respectively. A 1099-MISC will report any income you've received as an independent contractor.

See how simple that was? The IRS should hire me to teach people the tax code. I could be called the Tax Teacher.

Keep in mind that if you have any investments, those sources will provide you with forms after the end of the year that state how much your investments earned that year. And if you have a business, you'll need to file those taxes separately and refer to your own records to figure out your tax obligations.

Let's go into more detail now with respect to each of the pillars. Grab a cup of coffee or whatever else will help keep your eyes open, and let's get moving.

ORDINARY INCOME

Not everyone needs to file a tax return. If you're in the top 1%, your minions will file it for you. Okay, that is splitting hairs. You still have to file a tax return, although you can relax while the paid help do it. Also, they'll domicile you in some non-extradition offshore haven, so hey, $6.43 tax on $47 million sounds like a bargain. For the rest of us, if you're under 65, single, and have earned less than $12,400, you don't need to file a tax return. This limit changes to $24,800 for married couples filing jointly or a qualifying widow, and $18,650 for heads of households (Publication 17).

Regardless, there are some advantages to filing taxes. If you're in school, you may qualify for the education tax credit. People with low to moderate incomes may qualify for the earned income tax credit and health coverage tax credits as well. There are many calculators online that can tell you which, if any, credits you are eligible for. You'll also need to file a tax return if you have had tax withheld at source that you want to reclaim, and, for 2019 and 2020, you'll need to file to get the Corona Stimulus payment.

Ordinary income taxes are determined on the basis of tax brackets. The latest tax brackets can be found at https://taxfoundation.org/2020-tax-brackets/. Tax brackets change every year, so it's best to check for updates. The brackets look complex but are really quite simple. Everyone pays a certain percentage of their income as tax, depending on how much money they have earned and what their filing status is. Don't freak out though, you're not taxed on how much money you make, you're taxed on the amount *after* deductions and exemptions. I'm coming to that in a bit. You can wipe that sweaty forehead and breathe a sigh of relief now. Here's another nice table for you. The brackets range from 10% to 37%.

Tax Rates	Single Individuals Tax Bracket	Married, Filing Jointly Tax Bracket	Head of Household Tax Bracket	Married Filing Separately Tax Bracket
10%	$0–$9,875	$0–$19,750	$0–$14,100	$0–$9,875
12%	$9,876–$40,125	$19,751–$80,250	$14,101–$53,700	$9,876–$40,125
22%	$40,126–$85,525	$80,251–$171,050	$53,701–$85,500	$40,126–$85,525
24%	$85,526–$163,300	$171,051–$326,600	$85,501–$163,300	$85,526–$163,300
32%	$163,301–$207,350	$326,601–$414,700	$163,301–$207,350	$163,301–$207,350
35%	$207,351–$518,400	$414,701–$622,050	$207,351–$518,400	$207,351–$311,025
37%	$518,401 or more	$622,051 or more	$518,401 or more	$311,026 or more

Table 2: Federal Income Tax Brackets for 2020 (El-Sibaie, 2019)

You can file as a single individual, a married couple (filing jointly or separately), or as a head of household. The income limits for each bracket differ depending on the filing status. For example, single individuals pay 10% taxes on income between zero and $9,875. However, married couples filing jointly pay 10% taxes on income up to $19,750.

A key point to note here is that the US adopts an incremental tax system. Here's how it works. Let's say you're single and earning $50,000 per year. Looking at the table above, this falls into the 22% tax bracket. However, that doesn't mean you'll pay 22% of $50,000 in taxes. Instead, your income will be broken down according to the brackets.

The $50,000 can be broken down as follows: $9,875 + $40,125.

You'll therefore pay 10% of $9,875 and 12% of $40,125. That results in a total tax bill of $5,802.50, which is just 11.6% of your income. With me so far?

That's all there really is to figuring out your ordinary income tax rate. Note that your income earned can reduce depending on the deductions you take. It can also increase based on the nature of your investments. For example, if you have a side business that you draw salary from, that can increase your earned income. Interest earned on your savings accounts also counts toward your taxable income. You'll learn more about deductions shortly. For now, it's time to look at capital gains tax.

CAPITAL GAINS TAX

Those gains in the gym? Capital! Unfortunately, not the capital gains we're discussing here when the IRS steals from taxes any increases in your investments. There are two types of capital gains: long-term and short-term. Any investment or asset that you hold onto for more than a year is usually considered a long-term asset, although there are some exceptions. Selling such an asset for a profit triggers long-term capital gain. If you sell it after holding it for less than a year, that's a short-term capital gain. Short-term capital gains taxes are the same as ordinary income taxes.

That is to say that short-term capital gains are treated as ordinary income. Long-term capital gains are treated differently. These taxes have just three brackets that range from 0% to 20%. These rates are much lower than the ordinary income tax rates. The bracket you fall into depends on your filing status and taxable income earned, not the size of your capital gain.

Rate	Single	Married, filing jointly	Married, filing separately	Head of household
0%	Up to $40,000	Up to $80,000	Up to $40,000	Up to $53,600
15%	$40,001 – $441,450	$80,001 – $496,600	$40,001 – $248,300	$53,601 – $469,050
20%	Over $441,450	Over $496,600	Over $248,300	Over $469,050

Table 3: Long-Term Capital Gains Taxes for 2020 (El-Sibaie, 2019)

Take a look at the table below as an example. Let's assume you bought 50 shares in the stock market at $10 per share. The investment cost you $500. You then sold those 50 shares more than a year later for $20 per share, making a total of $1,000. Your capital gain in this case is $1,000 – $500 = $500. If you're single and earning $40,001, your long-term gains are taxed at

15%. 15% of $500 = $75. That's all you need to pay in capital gains taxes.

The tax advantages of holding on to investments for more than a year are immense. One thing to note, however, is that some states (such as California) don't have a Capital Gains rate at all and charge everything at ordinary tax rates.

50 shares bought @$10/share	$500
50 shares sold @$20/share	$1,000
Capital gain	$1,000 − $500 = $500
Tax paid	15% of $500 = $75

DEDUCTIONS AND CREDITS

Now this is where the good stuff begins! At long last, we get to take some money back! The final pillar of your taxes is deductions and credits. These lower your taxable income and reduce your tax bill. There are two broad categories of deductions. The first is the standard deduction. This is a single amount that you can automatically deduct from your income. In 2020, this amount was $12,400 for single filers, $24,800 for married filers, and $18,650 for heads of household. For example, if you earned $60,000 and are filing as an individual, you can immediately subtract $12,400 from $60,000 and pay tax only on $47,600 ($60,000 − $12,400) (Orem, 2020).

The second type of deduction is called an itemized deduction. These are individual deductions you can claim. There's a catch, though. The IRS allows you to claim **either** the standard deduction *or* itemized deductions. It makes sense, therefore, to itemize your deductions only if their sum is greater than the standard deduction. The IRS will ask for proof of each itemized deduction you claim. Below are a few examples of itemized deductions:

- Mortgage interest
- Student loan debt interest
- Deductions for state and local taxes
- Medical expenses
- Charitable donations

Good news, though. There are certain deductions, referred to as above-the-line deductions, that you can take even if you claim the standard deduction. An above-the-line deduction is an item that is subtracted directly from your gross income to arrive at your adjusted gross income (AGI). Here's the formula:

Gross income – above-the-line deductions = AGI

By contrast, below-the-line deductions are subtracted from your AGI once that amount has been determined. The standard deduction and the itemized deductions listed above are all below the line.

AGI – below-the-line deductions = taxable income

Here is a list of some above-the-line deductions (Berry-Johnson, 2020):

- Educator expenses
- Certain business expenses of reservists, performing artists, and fee-based government officials
- Health savings account (HSA) contributions
- Moving expenses for members of the Armed Forces
- The deductible portion of self-employment taxes
- Contributions to self-employed IRAs
- Self-employed health insurance premiums
- Penalties on early savings withdrawals
- Alimony paid
- Deductible contributions to IRAs
- Student loan interest
- For 2020, due to Coronavirus, up to $300 of charitable contributions are above-the-line

Unlike deductions, which only lower AGI, tax credits directly lower your final tax bill. They offset your final tax payable dollar for dollar. So it's definitely worth doing your research on this before filing a tax return. The individual eligibility requirements of these tax credits will vary, so it's best to check with the IRS or a qualified accountant.

Here are some of the most claimed credits (Orem, 2020):

- American Opportunity tax credit – This is a credit available to eligible students in the first four years of higher education. You can receive up to $2,500 per year.
- Lifetime Learning credit – This credit was created to promote education. To claim this, you must be paying qualified higher education expenses and must be enrolled at an eligible educational institution. The credit is worth 20% of the first $10,000 you spend on your education.
- Earned Income tax credit – This credit is available for people with low to moderate incomes. The credit amount changes each year.
- Saver's credit – If you make salary deferral contributions to your retirement accounts, you can be eligible for up to $1,000 in Saver's credit per year (or $2,000 if filing jointly).

That's all there is to deductions and credits.

CALCULATING TAXES AND FILING YOUR RETURNS

Let's walk through an example to see how you can calculate your taxes. For the purposes of this example, we'll assume you're a regular US taxpayer working a regular job with no complicated side businesses or investments.

As explained above, your employer will ask you to fill out form W-4, which specifies the amount of your income to be withheld for tax purposes. They'll take that form, calculate the amount to be withheld, deduct that amount from your paycheck, and send it to the IRS. When you file your taxes, your withheld amount is deducted from the taxes you owe. At the end of the year, your employer will provide you with Form W-2, which lists your wages earned and the amount of taxes withheld. **Below are the steps you would take to calculate and file your taxes:**

Step 1: Obtain your W-2. We will use the gross income figure from your W-2. Let's say it is $60,000.

Step 2: Get Form 104o and record your income. Next, record your above-the-line deductions such as paying student loan interest or contributions to IRAs or self-employed qualified plans. Let's say these deductions add up to $12,000 for the year.

Step 3: Calculate your Adjusted Gross Income (AGI). This is arrived at by subtracting your above-the-line deductions from your wages. In this case it is $60,000 minus $12,000, which is $48,000.

Step 4: The next step is to subtract the standard deduction (or an itemized list) from your AGI. Assuming you're single and making a standard deduction, you'll subtract $12,400. In this case, that works out to $48,000 minus $12,400, which is $35,600. This is your taxable income.

Step 5: Now it's time to put this amount in the appropriate tax bracket. Here's how $35,600 would break down across the brackets:

10% tax on $9,875 = $987.50

12% tax on $25,725 = $3,087.00

That results in a tax bill of $4,074.50.

Step 6: Time to factor in tax credits. Let's say you are eligible for $1,000 in American Opportunity tax credit.

That brings your tax bill down to $3,074.50 ($4,074.50 – $1,000).

Step 7: Check your W-2 to determine how much was withheld by your employer. The amount of tax withheld according to your W-2 form will be deducted from your final tax bill. Sometimes you can end up having too much tax withheld, in which case you'll receive a tax refund. If too little is withheld, you'll have to pay the difference when it's time to file your tax return.

Step 8: To file a return, you will need to fill out Form 1040 and mail it to the IRS. You can use software such as TurboTax to figure out how much you'll need to pay, or hire an accountant or tax professional to do it for you. Some software programs allow you to file online for free if your filing requirements are simple. Make sure you file your taxes on time. The IRS charges you a late filing fee of 5%, which can rise to 25% of your unpaid taxes. It's best to file your taxes even if you can't afford to pay. You can always work out a payment plan with the IRS. Sample tax forms are available for download directly from the IRS website. Every form has a list of instructions attached to it that will help you understand how to fill them in.

The links are provided below:

- https://www.usa.gov/get-tax-forms
- https://www.irs.gov/pub/newsroom/1040a.pdf

Step 9: If you have bank accounts or assets outside the US, these may need reporting too.

UK TAXES

Enough with US taxes and on to the UK! You didn't think you were exempt, did you? Taxes in the UK work a bit differently, even though they're founded on the same pillars. Just like the US, the UK adopts an incremental tax system. The UK's brackets begin with a minimum amount of GBP 12,500 (unless you earn over £100,000 in which case it is reduced by £1 for every £2 you earn over £100k). This means that someone earning £50,000 is taxed 20% of £37,500, not 20% of £50,000. You'll need to pay tax on any benefits your employer provides such as housing allowances, vehicle allowances, and other compensation.

The tax year is also different from the US. In the US, the tax year is the same as the calendar year, whereas in the UK, the tax year runs from April 6 to April 5 of the following year.

Unlike the US where (almost) everyone files a return, in the UK most people don't. You only need to file in certain circumstances, and most employees on PAYE don't have to file. What is PAYE, you ask? The Pay As You Earn (PAYE) system is used to administer taxes. Your national insurance contributions and taxes are deducted before your salary is paid out to you. Here are the tax rates:

England/Wales and NI	Taxable Income	Tax Rate
Personal allowance	Up to £12,500	0%
Basic rate	£12,500–50,000	20%
Higher rate	£50,001–150,000	40%
Additional rate	£150,001+	45%

Table 4: England, Wales and Northern Ireland Tax Bands ("How to File Income Taxes in the UK")

Welsh rates are set by the Welsh government. For the current year they happen to be the same as English rates, but likely to diverge in the future.

Scotland has different tax bands, as illustrated in Table 5 below.

Tax Band Name	Taxable Income	Tax Rate
Personal Allowance	Up to £12,500	0%
Starter rate	Over £12,501 to £14,585	19%
Basic rate	Over £14,585 to £25,158	20%
Intermediate rate	Over £25,158 to £43,430	21%
Higher rate	Over £43,430 to £150,000	41%
Top rate	Over £150,000	46%

Table 5: Scotland Tax Bands ("How to File Income Taxes in the UK")

If you're self-employed or fulfill some other conditions (listed below), you'll need to complete an income tax self-assessment. The deadline for filing a paper return is October 31. If you're filing electronically, you'll need to file by January 31 of the following year. Here are the self-assessment conditions ("How to File Income Taxes in the UK"):

1. If you're self-employed earning over GBP 1,000 per year
2. If you're involved in a business partnership
3. If you're earning more than GBP 50,000 a year and received the Child Benefit
4. If you earn untaxed income such as tips, allowances, property rentals, and so on

You can file form SA100 by clicking on this link: http://www.gov.uk/log-in-file-self-assessment-tax-return.

Deductions are treated very differently in the UK, as is income derived from dividends and rental properties. Rental income is treated the same as other income, although dividends are taxed at a different rate. It's best to consult a tax advisor for the latest advice.

Generally speaking, pension and charity contributions are exempt from taxes. Unlike in the US, where married couples can file jointly, in the UK everyone must file individually. However married couples and those in civil partnerships can, in some cases, transfer some of the Personal Allowance from the higher earner to the lower. You can check the full list of applicable benefits on the government's website.

ACTION PLAN – DAYS 22–25

- When are you due to file taxes? Check and note this date.
- Consult a tax professional to determine which exemptions, deductions, and credits you qualify for.
- Familiarize yourself with tax forms. The links are provided below.

https://www.gov.uk/self-assessment-forms-and-helpsheets
https://www.usa.gov/get-tax-forms
https://www.irs.gov/pub/newsroom/1040a.pdf

HAVE MORE THAN ONE GOLDEN GOOSE – WHY YOU NEED MULTIPLE INCOME STREAMS

"Your economic security does not lie in your job; it lies in your own power to produce – to think, to learn, to create, to adapt. That's true financial independence. It's not having wealth; it's having the power to produce wealth."

— STEPHEN COVEY

G rowing up, people would ask me, "What do you want to be when you're older?" I never knew what to say. I know that's just a question adults ask because there isn't much else to say to an awkward 10-year-old kid, but *damn*, I felt the pressure. I knew the expectation was to say doctor, lawyer, or some other traditional and well-respected profession. So I usually just picked one of those at random. But the truth was that I just wanted to be like my mommy who was a full-time housewife doing charitable work in her free time and my daddy who worked only a few hours a week.

Society encourages us to go to school, get a good job, put some money away for retirement, and then stop working at age 65. It doesn't tell us what to do when we lose our job due to advances in automation, economic fluctuations, political uncertainty, and even the occasional global pandemic.

Or what if you just don't want to work for the rest of your life? What if you'd much rather stay home and play Monopoly with the kids?

How did my parents weather those storms and come out unscathed?

The answer is simple: They had multiple streams of income that diversified their income risk. A stable second income is an insurance policy at worst and an opportunity creator at best. With multiple streams of income, you'll be far better equipped to deal with the way the world is constantly changing.

So I learned from them, and while I was working in finance, I was also investing in the stock market and real estate, setting up my own digital marketing agency and writing this book. I left my job (no longer the bastion of permanence it used to be) once I found my passions lay elsewhere.

Find your second, or more, income streams, and you might even find your calling like I did.

THE NEED FOR MULTIPLE INCOME STREAMS

Did you know the average millionaire has seven income streams ("The 7 Income Streams of Millionaires")? Not only do they have seven streams, these streams are diversified so if one stream goes belly up, another exists to provide income. If you still aren't convinced, here are the top six reasons why having multiple income streams is important.

Security

The markets, stocks, and jobs are volatile, and they fluctuate. They can throw nasty surprises at you, and you need to be prepared for that at all times. Think of it this way: If you had a second source of income that was equal to your day job, would you be worried about losing your job? I don't think so.

Live Better but Still within Your Means

Everyone likes the finer things in life. However, if you're earning $4,000 per month, your budget may not have room for impromptu vacations or designer shoes. If you were earning $10,000 a month, though, you could dream some more.

Faster Wealth Creation

You played around with compounding earlier in this book. You learned that if you contributed $12,000 per year to an investment that returned 8% every year, you'd have close to $1 million in 25 years. What if you contributed twice that amount? With a yearly contribution of $24,000, you'd have close to $2 million, all in the same amount of time. An additional stream of income will allow you to make more, save more, and earn larger returns on your money.

Retire Early

Who really wants to keep working full-time till age 65? With time, your priorities are likely to shift. You'll want more time for yourself and your family. The fastest way to early retirement is making more money and growing it through investments. Having multiple streams of income provides you with the extra cash to invest and the added flexibility to take risks when investing.

Avoid Debt

All the cash you accumulate can be invested in buying an asset that can give you even more cash. You won't need to assume debt to finance these purchases, and that's what truly powers your wealth in a safe manner. You'll soon find yourself able to pay off your mortgage, vehicle, and credit cards. That will save you tons of money in interest, and you'll be well on your way to financial freedom.

Find Your Calling

Do you really love your job? Do you wake up every morning looking forward to the workday? A lot of us end up working in jobs we don't enjoy just to pay the bills. What's stopping you from doing some freelance work on the side or starting up a business? You have your income to support you. Use that time to test the waters and find what you are passionate about. By building multiple sources of income, you're exposing yourself to the wide array of opportunities out there to make a living. Somewhere along the way, you might find the one thing that truly makes you happy. And hopefully it makes you some cash, too!

CHARACTERISTICS OF A GOOD SECOND SOURCE OF INCOME

Not every source of income is created equally. So you need to evaluate your options carefully. The idea of creating a second source of income isn't to replace your active income completely. It might, which would be awesome, but that's not required. The goal is to have two sources of income running side by side. The first quality to look for in a second source of income is flexibility. It should be something you can work at in your extra hours without taking too much time away from your day job.

You also want it to be something that is scalable. For example, you might have earned a lot of money once by painting artwork for a particularly wealthy person with very unique taste. However, is this a scalable source of income? It could very well be with licensing of prints, calendars, and so on. And if that's where your passion and talents lie, that's great. But this type of second income will be more difficult to manage. Art is extremely subjective, and it can take decades to build a name for yourself. Who knows if other people of the same financial stature will appreciate that style? Compare this to a side hustle such as editing content online. Everyone needs content edited, thanks to the explosion of digital marketing. It's a highly in-demand skill. You can edit content yourself or even outsource work on freelancer websites.

You want the source of income to sustain itself without your efforts being needed all the time. That is why outsourcing is so powerful. Let's say you've decided to edit content but cannot find the time to take on more work. What if you could outsource work to freelancers who can do just as good a job as you? You can take on double the work and earn more. Even if you decide to take some time off, you can outsource work and continue to earn money.

The income source should also be something you enjoy doing. If you're miserable all the time, there's no point pursuing it. Find something that's fun to do and cheap to create. You don't want to be spending thousands creating a second source of income.

So what are good side hustle ideas? Let's take a look at some of them.

Freelance Services

Sites such as Fiverr and Upwork are great sources for you to find clients who need things done. You can literally offer any service on these websites. For example, there's someone offering to teach people to telepathically communicate with their pets. Don't ask me how I know that. There are also people offering psychic services to get their exes back. And there's a guy who will throw a message in a bottle into the ocean for you.

However, there are also people offering serious high-quality services on these websites. There are other freelance websites such as Freelancer.com and Toptal that are also great options. Toptal is geared toward computer programming and is full of skilled freelance developers. If you have any computer development skills, you can register there and earn money on the side. Graphic design, content writing, editing, and Photoshop skills are always in great demand.

Creating whiteboard videos and talking head explainer videos are also popular these days. Social media management is also an evergreen field since everyone needs help in that area. Take some time to look at some of the services being offered and the kinds of jobs being posted. You'll find that there's always something that fits your interests and skill set.

Selling Products

There's no limit to the things you can sell online. From baked goods to online courses to e-books—the sky's the limit! A good way to get started is to sell the stuff you don't need right now. Old clothes, shoes, and other possessions can earn you cash instead of gathering dust in your closet. Ebay, Craigslist, and Facebook Marketplace are great places for you to begin selling your stuff.

Once you're comfortable selling products through these websites, you might want to consider starting a business around them. One way to execute this plan is to attend estate sales and buy items for a cheap price. You can then resell them for higher prices. This is time-consuming, however, since you'll have to spend time traveling to and from these places. Instead, it's far better to practice what is called retail arbitrage.

Arbitrage is the act of buying a product for a price and selling that same product for a higher price on another medium. For example, you could buy something cheap on Amazon and resell it for a profit on eBay. This business model has been around for ages, and these days, it's easier than ever since nearly everything is online.

You can search for products on Amazon and compare them to auction prices on eBay. Doing this manually might take a lot of time, but there are tools that can help reduce your research time. Software such as Tactical Arbitrage, BuyBotPro, and SourceMogul help you narrow down listings that are mispriced between the two markets.

There are some additional steps you'll need to take. It's best to focus on items that are in high demand. How can you find such products? Thankfully, Amazon gives you this information for free. You can view a product's Best Sellers Rank (BSR) on the product page. The lower the number is, the better it sells. You can then plug this number into a tool such as the JungleScout's BSR sales estimator to figure out how much revenue you can expect by selling this item every month.

Add shipping and storage costs to your item, and you'll be able to figure out how much profit you can earn. Most retail arbitrage products have small spreads. The spread is the difference between the selling price and the purchase price. Smaller products tend to have smaller spreads. Their storage costs are low, and you'll need to sell them in bulk to be able to earn a profit. Bigger products have large spreads, but shipping and storing them are a bit of a hassle.

You might be wondering how to store and ship these items. You have some options here. The first is to sign up for Amazon's Fulfilled by Amazon (FBA) program. Using this, you can have your products shipped directly to Amazon's warehouses, and they'll take care of your shipping and handling. They will charge you a fee every month, and the structure is a bit complex, but you can take advantage of their massive traffic. You can use FBA even if you're not selling your product on Amazon.

The second option is to use a third-party fulfillment agency. These vendors store and ship your product and charge you fees, much like Amazon does. They'll charge you a lot less, and all you'll need to do is manage your product listing on Amazon or wherever else you choose to list it.

Use your retail arbitrage experience to build your own brand and sell your own products. You can evolve into a drop shipper.

Drop-Shipping

In the previous section, Selling Products, you didn't have to store your own products or ship them. All you were doing was locating a source, collecting orders, and having the product shipped to the customer. Drop-shipping works the same way except you're not arbitraging prices between two retail e-commerce websites. Instead, you're buying them from a whole-saler or manufacturer and reselling them to retail users.

The earlier days of drop-shipping were quite simple. Websites such as Alibaba made it easy to source Chinese suppliers of goods, and drop shippers set up one-page websites and ran ads on Facebook and Google. As the orders came in, the manufac-turer slapped a custom label onto the product and shipped the product to the customer. Shipping times were usually three to four weeks, if the product even arrived.

Customers soon caught wind of this, and now no one is willing to wait for more than a week for their products. The competi-tion is also much greater now as more and more people are starting drop-shipping businesses. To stand out from the crowd, you'll need to pick a niche that you can really make your own and pursue a targeted marketing strategy. Moreover, you'll likely need to have factories located close to your target customers in order to bring products to them quickly. In any case, American and British consumers have become very skeptical of products that have not been manufactured in their own countries. Both the quality of the product and the production practices adopted in third-world countries play a major role in this perception.

You'll need to spend time researching good products. Look at what sells on Amazon and check the Google search volume traffic for that product. Of course, it will take effort up front, but this business model satisfies all the criteria you may want for your secondary income source. You're not handling the products yourself and can outsource a lot of the work, making it scalable. If you pick a product niche you like, it's enjoyable. The time you spend on the business is entirely up to you. I'm not saying it's easy, but it's realistic to expect to build a business this way.

Drop-shipping can be extended to services as well. If there's enough demand for video editing services, for example, you can create a web page for this and hire freelancers to do the work for you. You can turn yourself into an agency.

Print on Demand

Print on demand (POD) is a great business to start these days because consumers are searching for more customization. POD services allow you to print designs on anything you want, including T-shirts, mugs, hoodies, leggings, tote bags, and so on. Amazon has a great service called Merch by Amazon that allows you to upload your designs on products that Amazon offers.

Websites such as Teespring offer you the same opportunity. The idea is that you'll create your own designs and then host them on either Teespring or Amazon. You can drive traffic to them by running Google or social media ads, depending on your budget. There are entire services around POD marketing, such as Placeit.

Using Placeit's software, you can superimpose your design on a model so it appears as if they're wearing your product. You can even create videos of them wearing your design. The software also has a rudimentary design interface you can use to quickly create new designs. If you have any graphic design skills, then selling POD merchandise is a great way to earn additional cash.

If you find that your designs are popular, you can expand your business to its own website using Shopify. You can host your designs on your website using Placeit's services and use a service such as Printful to fulfill your orders. They'll print and ship your orders for you so you don't need to worry about warehousing or fulfillment. Printful connects automatically to Shopify so you don't have to manually update anything.

All of this means you can devote time to setting up ads and creating designs. To further reduce your time burden, you can hire designers who can create designs based on your niche research. You'll know your customer well by this point so you'll be able to figure out what they want. This business is easily scalable since you can expand to printing on a wide array of products.

Play Video Games

Love video games? Well, then fire up your PlayStation! Playing video games was probably viewed as a less-than-productive use of your time when you were a kid, but it's big bucks these days. You can host a playthrough on Twitch and post the same video to YouTube. Gaming channels are extremely popular these days, and these videos receive high levels of engagement from viewers. Of course, you need to be very passionate about video games and be a highly skilled gamer to succeed with this method.

Twitch in particular is the largest gaming video host on the planet right now. It's flooded with playthroughs of every game imaginable. The best way to become popular on Twitch is to drive engagement. That means creating compelling playthroughs or even picking fights with popular gamers to generate attention. Think of it as rap battle tactics taken online. Everyone wins.

A popular niche that is expanding is the e-sports category. These video games are electronic versions of popular sports such as football, Formula One, basketball, and baseball. The opportunities are huge.

For example, the Formula One group posts replays of their e-sport races on their YouTube channel after the physical race is completed. There's even a championship that gamers can compete in. Madden (the NFL football franchise) has always hosted popular e-sports tournaments with finals in Las Vegas or New York's Times Square. E-sports have gone global, and gamers are attracting real sponsorship dollars.

Domain Flipping

Domain flipping is a business that has the potential to be extremely lucrative. Having said that, it's been around for a while, and people have picked up on it. However, there is increasing demand for websites, which means domain names are scarce. Even worse (or better for you), many website names are already taken. Imagine if you had bought the amazon.com domain back in 1995. Jeff Bezos would have paid an arm and a leg to buy that domain from you.

Or how about facebook.com? These are extreme examples, however, and it's unrealistic to expect to earn billions from domain name purchases. But you can earn a few hundred every month by buying and flipping domains. There are two approaches you can adopt.

The first is to focus solely on the domain name itself. A domain typically costs around $14.95 per year, so it isn't a huge expense. You can buy the domains you think have a good chance of being more valuable in the future. For example, superbowl70.com might be valuable down the road.

The best websites to flip domains on are Flippa.com and Reseller.com. You can purchase domains from other flippers or buy a domain from a website hosting provider such as Bluehost or GoDaddy and resell that domain on Flippa. This method isn't one that will generate massive income. However, if all you want is some money to cover your groceries each month, go for it.

The second approach to domain flipping requires more work but can land you a massive windfall. You can set up your own domain and then load it with relevant content that brings steady traffic. Most domain flippers focus on just the domain name and neglect to enhance the asset. That is why they don't get paid much unless they get lucky. By adding content and bringing in steady traffic, you're enhancing the asset and selling a working website instead of just a domain name.

Such assets sell for a lot more, and you'll be better compensated for your time. If you have the cash, you could even consider buying one of these domains and monetizing it with a product or a service. Let's say you find someone who's selling a domain related to VPNs. You could buy the website and monetize it by running ads on it or by recommending VPN providers who can pay you an affiliate commission. You could pay someone to write a book and sell it for $9.99 on your website. If 100 people buy your book, you've earned $1,000 for a single product.

Compare this to the previous method where you need to find domains over and over and will probably earn less than $100 per domain. It's unsustainable if you're looking at building this into a long-term business.

Blog/Content Creation

Starting a blog is the evergreen way of building a second income. The problem is that there's so much content on the web that it's quite hard to rank on Google's search. Their algorithm has also become more sophisticated, and if you happen to operate in a crowded niche, you're going to have a hard time ranking for anything unless you can display authority.

However, it's far from impossible to create a great web asset for yourself. That's how you ought to view your website or content outlet. It's an asset much like your property is an asset, and it can be monetized in different ways. In fact, web assets can be monetized in far more varied ways than real estate assets. It all begins with niche selection. When selecting a niche, you need to find the sweet spot between a large audience and a lack of competition. It's unrealistic to expect zero competition, but you don't want to compete in any niche that has behemoths operating in it. For example, if you decided to cover all of football, how can you expect to compete against ESPN, Sky, or any other major broadcaster?

Niche research is best conducted by looking at Google's Keyword Tool and Google Trends. This will let you know what the demand is like. The keyword tool will alert you to keywords within your niche, and Trends will let you know how search volume has been changing over time. You want niches that are stable or increasing. Get to know some of your competitors and look at the kind of content they're publishing. You can even start leaving responses to their content and build a relationship. That will come in handy down the road.

You can either set up a blog or a YouTube channel. Choosing YouTube will help you rank faster, but you won't own your audience. You should aim to build your own website so you have a place where you can collect user e-mails. If you're worried about appearing on camera, you can always record voice-over videos or create animated videos using software such as Powtoon or Animaker.

Collecting user e-mails is essential for success. You can't hope to succeed if you don't get to know your users better. Running newsletters to their e-mails and alerting them of new content is a great way to get them to return to your content and engage with it. Once you've built enough trust with them, you can monetize your content channels or release a product of your own. Affiliate marketing is also a great way to monetize your content. Affiliate marketing is when you publicize someone else's product in your content and earn commissions for the sales you'll generate.

There are a few other things you can do to boost your presence on the web. Collaborate with other influencers in your niche and see if they're interested in working with you. You can write guest posts for them or create content for or with them. If the influencer in your niche happens to be extremely popular, you can interview them, which is a nice ego boost for them and will help increase your online exposure, too.

Starting a successful content business is a topic in itself, and there are many nuances to it. It's tough, but in most cases your work will be heavily concentrated up front. Once your snowball gets rolling, it'll sustain itself with minimal effort.

Uber, Airbnb, and the Sharing Economy

The sharing or gig economy offers many ways for you to monetize your assets. The catch is that you need to have assets to begin with. For example, buying a car just to drive for Uber doesn't make sense. If you have a car, you can earn additional cash with it by driving for Uber. You can also monetize your car by picking up jobs where you deliver groceries or pizza.

If you have a house or apartment, you can lease it on Airbnb and earn additional cash. Always check to see if your landlord is comfortable with this idea. You can rent a two-bedroom apartment and rent the second bedroom for a higher price than what you are paying for the entire apartment. If you own your property, this method will be really easy to implement.

Stock Market Investing

Investing in the stock market is a no-brainer. Everyone needs to be doing this. You will learn all about it in the next chapter.

ACTION PLAN – DAYS 26–27

- How would you like to make money? Make a list of 10 ideas at the very least. Consider your interest, skills, and the amount of free time you have available. This should help narrow down your list. Remember, the more passion you have for something, the more likely it will be lucrative for you. But it's also important to be practical. Conduct your own research online since there is so much out there. This chapter is by no means an exhaustive list.

- Implement two methods immediately. You won't earn money right off the bat. However, with time and determination, it'll come. If you find a particular method unappealing, then ditch it for the next one on your list. Start small with odd jobs or Fiverr gigs and work your way up.

"At least eighty percent of millionaires are self-made. That is, they started with nothing but ambition and energy, the same way most of us start."

— BRIAN TRACY

MAKE YOUR MONEY WORK FOR YOU – BASICS OF INVESTING

"If you don't find a way to make money while you sleep, you will work until you die."

— WARREN BUFFETT

So far in this book, I've discussed how you can make money, save money, and then pay some of that money to the government. It's time to shift your focus from working for money to making it work for you.

Unfortunately, fewer than half of young Americans have invested money in stocks (Carter, 2018). Why is that? With an average annual return of 10%, investing in the stock market should be a no-brainer (Royal, 2020). And my friend Buffet agrees. But here are the top three objections I hear:

1. I'm scared of losing all my money.
2. It seems so complicated. I don't know where to start.
3. My money is probably safer in a bank.

Let me deal with each of them one by one

1. Stock prices will fluctuate on a day-to-day basis, and market returns will vary each year as well. But investing is a long-term game. If you only focus on short-term results, you'll always be fearful. Remember that the historical average return is 10%.
2. You've made a start already. You've reached the end of this book. Once you understand some of the basic investing concepts and terminology, you'll realize it's not as difficult as you thought. Start small if you're nervous. Try investing just $50 and see how you feel.
3. The dollar loses about 2% of its value each year to inflation. To offset inflation, you should only keep a small amount of money in your checking account to cover daily expenses. The rest should be in a high-yield savings account (HYSA) and investment accounts.

Check out the graph below, which demonstrates the returns you would make on a $20,000 investment over a 30-year period if you left the money under your mattress, in a regular savings account, in a HYSA, or invested in the stock market. Please note that this is for illustration purposes only, and the actual rates of return will vary significantly depending on economic conditions, the banks you use, and the investment strategy you adopt.

For regular savings accounts, the FDIC claims the average interest rate is currently 0.05%, so we'll use that ("Weekly National Rates"). By contrast, high-yield savings accounts can earn around 0.5% (Burnette, 2021). I have assumed an 8% return for the stock market, slightly lower than the historical average.

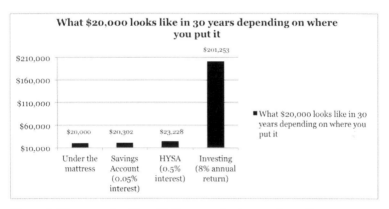

Figure 1: Money under Your Mattress vs. Savings vs. Investing (Goldman).

Credit to Wealthsimple for the idea of the above graph. However, please note that different numbers were used in my version to reflect a more accurate rate of return.

Look. At. That. Isn't it worth the risk for the returns you can realistically expect to achieve? In this chapter, I'm going to give you an introduction to the basic concepts of investing and an overview of the various methods of investment. This is just a starting point but more than enough to process for the purposes of this crash course. Before we do that, here is a little song I wrote just for you:

Invest, Invest, Invest
Don't Stress.
Let your money do the rest!

INVESTING 101

Before we go into detail about *how* to invest and *what* you can invest in, let's cover some basic investing terminology.

Opportunity Cost

Opportunity cost is the economic term for the phrase "nothing in life is free." When you choose to pursue an investment, you're giving up the opportunity to invest in something else. You're incurring a cost. The benefit you gain from your choice needs to be greater than your opportunity cost. Let's look at an example. Let's say you're presented with two choices of what to eat: chocolate cake or pancakes with maple syrup.

Both of them are delicious. Your choice comes down to which one makes you feel better. If you prefer breakfast food, you might go with the pancakes. If you prefer the fudgy texture of chocolate cake, then cake it is. You'll automatically weigh the pleasure derived from one option against the feeling of having lost the other option. We do this intuitively everywhere, be it with food, romantic partners, clothing choices, or accessories. Yet we don't do it with money.

We let our money sit in a checking account or a regular savings account because it's safer than investing in stocks. The graph above has already demonstrated the massive difference between these investment options. But let me reiterate this point. If we use the figures in the graph above, we can earn 891% more by investing in the stock market versus a regular savings account, with the same upfront investment and over the exact same period of time. Granted, there is more risk with the stock market, but is it worth taking that risk for a potential 891% increase in reward? That's the essence of evaluating opportunity cost.

Inflation

Inflation is an economic cost you incur all the time. It refers to how prices of goods in an economy keep increasing over time. The average inflation rate between 2010 and 2019 was 1.78% in the US and 2.88% in the UK ("Annual Inflation Rates in the United States"). As things get more expensive, your purchasing power decreases. That means you can buy fewer things with the same amount of money.

For example, if it costs you $500 to buy a flat screen TV today, it will cost you $600 next year, assuming a 2% inflation rate. In order to offset the loss from inflation, our investments should provide a rate of return higher than the rate of inflation at the time. That means your HYSA was losing you money by paying only 0.5% in interest. That doesn't mean you don't need one. We have covered the reasons why having such an account is necessary. But investing in the stock market is one of the best ways to ensure the value of your money doesn't erode over time.

Diversification

Diversification is finance-speak for "don't put all your eggs in one basket". If you drop that basket, all the eggs break. It's much safer to spread them out in three baskets. That way, there's a chance at least one will make it to the kitchen in time for breakfast!

That is what diversification does for the average investor. It allows you to spread your risk evenly across varied investment options, making it more likely you'll succeed in earning a profit at any given time. Diversification is, however, a thorny issue among professional investors. Warren Buffett and Mark Cuban in particular think that diversification makes little sense (Kiyosaki, 1998). But there's a caveat. Buffet says it doesn't make sense for someone who *knows* what they're doing. If you have the knowledge and the time to analyze individual businesses and you understand market trends, you're better off concentrating your portfolio on where you expect to receive the highest possible returns.

But the average investor does not have that kind of knowledge or time. For regular people like you and me, it makes much more sense to diversify—to play it safe. We'll cover how to do that later.

Indexes

Stock market performance is measured by looking at what their indexes are worth. An index is a mathematical average of a group of stocks that provides a quick and reliable snapshot of how the stock market is performing. For example, the UK stock markets are measured by the performance of the FTSE 100 (pronounced footsy), a collection of the 100 largest companies in the UK. Its equivalent in the US is the S&P 500 (this doesn't have a creative pronunciation), which is a collection of the 500 largest companies in the US all rolled up into one easily readable average price. There are other indexes such as the NASDAQ Composite and the Dow Jones Industrial Average, but the S&P 500 is the most widely used.

Anything that is a calculated average of many different components can be considered an index. You could create one yourself. It's unlikely anyone would pay much attention to it, though. Let's say you're a famous local baker. You decide to weigh 10 of your most popular cakes and calculate an average weight. That would be an index. If the weights of the cakes vary each time you bake, the index would change too. That's really all there is to it.

Exchanges

Exchanges are marketplaces. Much like how seafood is traded at wholesale markets, financial instruments are traded on exchanges. Popular exchanges include the FTSE (the UK stock index), the NYSE (New York Stock Exchange), and NASDAQ (both American).

Active vs. Passive Investing

Passive investing is a long-term investment strategy, whereas active investing is focused on short-term wins. Let's talk about active investing first.

Active investing is actively watching the market to find ideal buying and selling opportunities. Active investors make money by taking advantage of short-term stock market fluctuations. The goal of active investing is to outperform some sort of benchmark. A benchmark is an index or indices that indicate how the overall stock market is performing. The S&P 500 is an index of the 500 largest stocks in the US and is the most commonly used benchmark of overall stock market performance. So when you hear an investor say they're trying to beat the market, what they're trying to do is get higher investment returns than the S&P 500 Index.

Passive investing is when an investor adopts a buy-and-hold strategy as opposed to making regular trades. Passive strategies don't focus on short-term fluctuations in a stock's price. There is little to no research or analysis involved. Instead, investors put their money in a diversified fund, sit back, and let it grow over time.

Research shows that 89% of fund managers fail to beat the market over a 10-year period ("SPIVA U.S. Scorecard"). Fund managers are the experts. These are people who have dedicated their lives to learning about the stock market and identifying ideal investment opportunities. Think about how difficult it would be for us regular peeps to do this.

Passive investment, when carried out well, is far easier and has shown time and again to produce better results. Warren Buffett recommends investing in an index fund that tracks the S&P 500 and costs very little to manage. This chapter will show you how to do that.

LEARN TO PLAY THE RIGHT INSTRUMENTS

No, not the musical kind! These are some real money-making instruments. You see, investing in the stock market is carried out through financial instruments. Different instruments have different risk profiles and return characteristics. There are many out there, but here are the ones you need to focus on and learn about for now.

Stocks

Stocks and shares are used interchangeably and mostly represent the same thing. They're a slice of companies that trade on an exchange—hence the term *shares*. The ticker AMZN, for example, is an abbreviation that represents Amazon's publicly traded shares in the markets.

So why do stock prices fluctuate so much in the short term? If you've ever done an economics class, you'll know about supply and demand. I'll summarize. Supply and demand is a concept that explains how the prices of items in an economy are determined by the popularity of that particular item with the general public. When people want something (i.e., it's in high demand but supply is low), the price goes up. But when people don't want something (i.e., there's a low demand but a high supply), prices go down. That is exactly how stocks work.

But what influences supply and demand? The financial news, media, and social media play a huge part in the public's perception of a particular business or product. For example, you might have noticed how Tesla's stock seems to live and die with Elon Musk's tweets. If Musk were to leave us a drunken tweet about Tesla tomorrow, you can bet the price of Tesla stock would plummet. Or it might shoot up. It depends on how funny Musk is when he's drunk.

There are two ways to earn money with stocks. The first is through capital gains, and the second is through dividends (cash flow). If you sell a stock for a higher price than what you bought it for, that's a capital gain. Capital gains are not realized until you sell. Think of a football game that seesaws all the way to the final whistle. No one wins or loses until the whistle blows. Similarly, you don't incur gains or losses until you sell.

Companies can choose to pay a certain percentage of profits back to shareholders as cash distributions per share. This distribution is called a dividend. The dividend paid per share divided by the stock price is called the yield. The yield is the income or cash flow you earn from your investment. If a company pays $2 per share and if its stock sells for $100, its yield is 2%.

Companies such as Coca-Cola, Pepsi, and Nestlé usually pay dividends. These behemoths have been around for ages and have stable businesses with very few competitors. There's not much growth to be had, which is why it makes sense to pay shareholders back. A company like Amazon is still growing and needs money to purchase competitors. That is why it doesn't pay dividends. Keep that information in mind for later.

Pros of Stock Market Investing

- High liquidity – Investors can get into and out of stocks relatively quickly.
- Transparency – Public corporations have to release earning reports that tell investors how their company is performing. We all have access to this information.

- Potential – There is a potential to make a lot of money through dividend payments or capital gains.
- Comparatively small upfront investment – Unlike other investment avenues (e.g., real estate, bonds), you don't need lots of cash up front to start investing in stocks.

Cons of Stock Market Investing

- Volatility – Investors have to be prepared to deal with wild swings in the market.
- Information overload – There is too much conflicting information available on the Internet, which can be overwhelming for new investors. This often leads to emotional rather than rational investing.
- Risky – If the company you have invested in goes bankrupt, you typically won't receive anything.
- Returns – It is very difficult to achieve above-average market returns.

Bonds

We've built a great *bond* so far, haven't we? Ha. I make myself laugh. So what are bonds in the financial world? Bonds are another major instrument traded in the markets. And here's how a bond works. When a company issues a bond, they're asking for a loan from market participants. If you buy a bond, you're loaning them money that is equal to the face value of the bond you buy. A bond's face value is the price it initially sells for. This is fixed by the company.

In exchange for the money you give them, the company pays you an interest rate (called the coupon rate) for a certain term. Both of these are fixed by the company and are communicated when the bonds are issued. For example, a $1,000 face-value bond with a coupon of 5% and a term of 10 years will pay you 5% interest every year for every $1,000 bond purchase you make. At the end of 10 years, the bond reaches maturity. The investor redeems his bond, and you receive your $1,000 back.

Here's where it gets interesting. Once the bonds are issued, the company has the money it needs and proceeds to use it. The bonds you've bought trade on the markets just as stocks do. Their price fluctuates. That means the face value and price differ. You might have paid $1,000 for a bond, but it might be trading for $900 in the markets. Have you lost money? No. You'll lose money only if you sell your bond for that price.

Bond prices fluctuate based on perceptions of safety. If a company is likely to default on its payments, its bond prices will crash. Bond prices are quoted in percentages of the face value. A $1,000 face-value bond trading for $900 is quoted as 90. If a company defaults, prices crash to zero or single digits. If it pays on time and is highly rated, it might trade above 100.

That means you can earn capital gains on bonds despite them being primarily cash flow instruments. For example, you could buy a bond with 70 and hold it until maturity. You'll earn interest as well as a 30% capital gain since you'll receive 100% back on maturity. If you sell a bond, you're giving up your face value in exchange for whatever price you receive. Bonds have returned 5.1% annually over the past 100 years on average ("What's a Bond?"). The lower return is compensated by the income earned via interest.

Pros of Bonds

- Investment returns are fixed. Bonds are less volatile than stocks and will generate regular income for you through interest payments.
- You can also sell them before maturity and earn capital gains.
- All bonds are given investment ratings (ranging from AAA to D), which gives you a nice way to evaluate their investment worthiness.
- If the company goes bankrupt, you're a creditor and will receive something in return from the disbursal of the company's assets (although this isn't guaranteed and depends on the company's asset levels).

Cons of Bonds

- You won't earn capital gains with them for the most part. If a company does well, its stock will rise a lot higher.
- Companies usually refinance bonds when interest rates change. That means your money could be returned to you before you expect it to, and you will have to find new areas of investment.
- Bonds are typically pricier than the average stock, so there's a capital hurdle as well. They can range from $1,000 to $100,000.
- Bonds are less liquid compared to stocks (particularly if the bond is issued by a small and less financially stable company).

Real Estate Investment Trusts

I'm not covering real estate investment in this chapter, so what's this doing here? Real Estate Investment Trusts (REITs) are stocks that allow you to invest in real estate and earn dividend income. They yield much more than traditional common stock dividends for one reason. REITs need to pay 90% of their income back to shareholders. How does an REIT generate income?

It does so by managing large properties such as shopping centers, apartment buildings, and other complexes. The rent they earn is passed on to you as a shareholder, less whatever expenses the company incurs. Owning an REIT stock doesn't give you direct property ownership. However, you can earn income from real estate by owning these stocks.

Pros of REITs

- Provide you with steady cash flow and the ability to earn real estate income with a small investment.
- Allow you to gain exposure to the real estate market without paying a down payment or a large sum of money.
- Lets you diversify your real estate focus as much as you want.

Cons of REITs

- You won't own physical real estate but shares in the company that does.
- You'll earn 90% of the profits the company earns, which is not the same as rental income.
- If an REIT has high costs, your potential earnings as a proportion of rents collected will be low.

Funds

Funds are where the fun begins! As interesting as bonds and stocks are, they are risky and time-consuming for a beginner.

You need to be willing to spend time analyzing the prospects of a company and its ability to pay back shareholders and bond-holders (i.e., you). And even then, as statistics have shown, you're unlikely to beat the market. The flip side is that if you do it well, you can earn well above average market returns.

The how-to of investing in individual stocks is outside the scope of this book. There are many books that cover this in detail, such as *The Intelligent Investor* by Benjamin Graham. For now, my aim is to give you a simple and low-risk method, a passive investment strategy focused on investing in funds. There are three types of funds you can invest in. They are mutual funds, index funds, and exchange-traded funds (ETFs).

First, let's talk about mutual funds. Mutual funds have been around the longest. They were created as a way for people to pool their money and make investments together. Let's use a food analogy to explain this. Feel free to order some pizza before you dive into the next part. Nothing like some active, hands-on learning!

So let's say you order a pizza. Your pizza comes in a nice big cardboard box, right? That box is your mutual fund. Open the box, and you have 10 big cheesy slices inside. Yum. But hold on! They're all different! Each slice has a different base and a different set of toppings. There's good old-fashioned pepperoni, some boring plain cheese, and they even had the audacity to add pineapple! *Why did the pizza guy do this?* You ask yourself. Well, he wanted to reduce the risk of your hating the pizza by diversifying. Excuse my French, but he was saving his own a**. A mutual fund is a way to take a whole lot of stocks that are out there and package them in one little box. You put your money into one box, and you've diversified your investment without having to worry about multiple individual assets.

Mutual funds are generally managed by a professional in exchange for a fee. They are professional stock pickers who buy and sell stocks over time to try to beat the market average. Most mutual funds aim to outperform the market, but most of them fail to do so (Gresham). However, they offer you a way to capture market outperformance *if* you pick the right fund.

Let's summarize.

Pros of Mutual Funds

- You can own a bunch of different stocks all in one easy package. You only need to make one purchase.
- They are diversified. Owning lots of different stocks at once reduces your investment risk.
- Professional management allows you to outsource your investing portfolio and let someone else handle it for you.
- They're actively managed and can potentially deliver above-average market returns.

Cons of Mutual Funds

- Most mutual funds underperform the market.
- They have higher fees compared to other options. Your total annual fees with a mutual fund can exceed 2% (Berger, 2020). Even if the fund manager made bad investment decisions, a fixed percentage of your investment goes to him.

Index funds, by contrast, don't aim for outperformance. Index funds are a type of mutual fund. These funds aim for the market average by replicating the holdings in an index. They completely eliminate the need for a human being to make buying and selling decisions. A computer tracks the market to match the stock market index it's following. For example, an index fund tracking the S&P 500 will hold all the stocks in that index, and it'll perform pretty much as the index does. If the index rises by 8% every year on average, it'll do the same. Index funds are generally cheaper due to the low costs of running a passive fund with no human intervention.

ETFs are very similar to index funds, with one key difference. Index funds can only be bought or sold at the end of the trading day, when their price is set. ETFs, on the other hand, are traded like stock. They can be bought or sold throughout the day, whenever the stock market is open. Also, not all ETFs track indexes (though there are many that do).

Pros of Index Funds

- As with mutual funds, you make one purchase and get a diversified portfolio.
- They're cheaper than the average mutual fund.
- They're simple and easy to invest in.
- They can deliver average market returns (which is still a lot).

Cons of Index Funds

- They're priced just once per day, so you could potentially get a less than optimal price compared to market conditions.
- You'll earn average returns, which means you can't outperform the market.
- Some funds have minimum investment requirements of $3,000 or more.

Pros of ETFs

- Make one purchase and get a diversified portfolio.
- They're priced just like common stocks so their prices match their portfolio value. That means you'll receive fair prices almost always.
- There are no investment minimums, and you can buy as little as one unit.

- You earn average market returns.

Cons of ETFs

- Not all ETFs follow indexing strategies. If you buy one that aims for outperformance, you'll pay more fees potentially than with a mutual fund.

The best way to passively invest in the stock market is to buy an index fund or ETF that tracks dividend-paying stocks or broad stock market indexes. Reinvest any dividends you earn and buy even more fund units. In exchange, index funds and ETFs will charge you low fees, usually less than 0.05% of your investment, every year ("Expect High-Quality, Low-Cost ETFs"). Compare that to 1% or more for mutual funds. You can buy a fund that tracks stocks, one that tracks bonds, and another that tracks REITs. And you've got yourself a pretty balanced portfolio.

Note that your investment won't earn 8% every year like clockwork. Here is how the stock market performed from 2008 to 2019:

Year	Return
2019	31.49%
2018	-4.38%
2017	21.83%
2016	11.96%
2015	1.38%
2014	13.69%
2013	32.39%
2012	16.00%
2011	2.11%
2010	15.06%
2009	26.46%
2008	-37%

Table 6: S&P 500 Return from 2008–2019

There are some astonishing years, and there are depressing ones as well. The key is to keep holding on for the long term. That is why getting rich slowly works. If you actively jumped in and out in this period, you could have made a lot of money. However, how tough would that have been to constantly analyze the markets, try to predict them, and so on. You'd have also been hit with short-term capital gains taxes for all that work, reducing your overall gain significantly.

It's easier to buy and hold. Warren Buffett and Charlie Munger recommend this, so who are we to suggest otherwise?

INVESTMENT ACCOUNTS

So we've covered *what* to invest in, now let's talk about the *how*. You need to open an investment account. Broadly, there are two types of investment accounts to be aware of, if you live in the US. I'll cover the UK later.

1. Standard Brokerage Account

A standard brokerage account is a "regular" investment account, or a non-retirement account. With these accounts you gain access to a wide range of investments including stocks, mutual funds, index funds, ETFs and bonds. Any interest or dividends earned, as well as any gains made, are taxed as normal. There are many reputable brokers you can open an account with, such as Charles Schwab or Fidelity.

2. Retirement Accounts

Retirement accounts are very similar. And you can invest in the same financial instruments. These accounts help you put money away for retirement and allow that money to compound over time. The key difference between a retirement account and a standard brokerage account is the tax benefits you receive. Ideally, you should only contribute to standard brokerage accounts after your retirement accounts are maxed. I'll cover the tax advantages in detail below. There are 3 main retirement accounts to be aware of: 401(k), Traditional IRA, Roth IRA.

Here's briefly how these retirement accounts work:

1. 401(k) – You can contribute up to $19,500 per year in a 401(k), and you can withdraw from these accounts once you're 59-1/2 years old. These accounts are provided by your employer, and best of all, most employers will match a percentage of your contributions. Moreover, any contributions you make are pre-tax and therefore reduce your taxable income. It's a win-win situation. Get your hands on some free money *and* pay less taxes. Woohoo! Make sure you max your contributions every year, particularly if your employer is matching them. Employers set different rules with regard to matching contributions and withdrawal requirements, so make sure you clarify this. You can also open a solo 401(k). That is especially useful if you're self-employed. You can make contributions as an employer and as an employee. Check with an accountant to understand how these work.

2. Individual Retirement Account (IRA) – This is an account you can open and fund yourself. You can only contribute to an IRA if you have what the IRS calls "earned" income. Weird, right? You'd think all income was "earned". Anyway, the IRS begs to differ. If you have a salary or commission from a job or make money from a business you run, that's earned income.

However, any investment income from rental properties or other assets doesn't count. That's apparently
unearned. There are a few other nuances (e.g., child
support doesn't count, but disability benefits do).
Always check the specifics on the IRS website or with a
tax professional.

You can contribute $6,000 per year to this account
($7,000 if you're 50 or older) from pre-tax income and
not pay any taxes on gains until you withdraw your
money at the age of 59-1/2 or older. The combined
annual contribution limit for both traditional and Roth
IRAs is $6,000. The only downside is if you or your
spouse already have a 401(k), the IRS decides to reduce
the amount of contributions that are tax-deductible.
That depends on your income levels, though. For example, in 2020, if you are single and earning $65,000 or
less, you'll still get a full deduction even with a 401(k). If
you're making more than that, things change. Check out
the IRS website for more details on the income limits
that apply. Also, don't forget that withdrawing prior to
age 59-1/2 will cost you a penalty of 10% plus taxes.

3. Roth IRA – This is an account you can open and
fund yourself, too, provided you have earned income.
Good old Roth doesn't have any minimum age threshold
or limit, which is great. If you're a teenager with a job at
the local fried chicken shop, you may as well start

contributing to a Roth IRA. You may need parental or custodial approval for this until you're a certain age, but it's worth looking into.

You can contribute $6,000 per year ($7,000 if you're age 50 or older) from taxable income. Since you're contributing with after-tax dollars, you won't receive an immediate tax deduction benefit. However, once you're 59 ½ and have had the account for five years, both your contributions and earnings can be withdrawn tax-free. Pretty awesome, right?

Unlike the traditional IRA, your ability to contribute reduces once you hit certain income levels. For example, if you are single and earn $124,000 or more per year, you won't be allowed to contribute as much. However, in this case, the IRS doesn't care if you have a 401(k) already, and that doesn't impact your contributions. Remember that $6,000 is the combined annual contribution limit for both traditional and Roth IRAs. Always check the IRS website for details on income limits.

As I mentioned above, withdrawals can be made from the age of 59 ½ and after you have had the account for five years. However, there are a few situations where the IRS allows you to withdraw the money in your Roth IRA **before age 59 ½** or if you've had the account for **less than five years**, without penalty. These conditions are as follows ("Roth IRA Withdrawal Rules"):"

- You use the withdrawal (up to a $10,000 lifetime maximum) to pay for a first-time home purchase.
- You use the withdrawal to pay for qualified education expenses.
- You use the withdrawal for qualified expenses related to a birth or adoption.
- You become disabled or pass away.
- You use the withdrawal to pay for unreimbursed medical expenses or health insurance if you're unemployed.
- You agree to receive the payments in roughly equal amounts over a five-year period or until you reach 59-1/2 years old (whichever is longer) in order to avoid the penalty.

Traditional vs. Roth IRA

You must be thinking, *How many of these accounts do I need? If I have a 401(k) and my employer is sorting that out, I can ignore the rest of this, right?* Nope. Do you want to spend your retirement years traveling the world and enjoying lavish meals with your significant other? Invest in both a 401(k) and an IRA. Your employer-sponsored 401(k) will be limited in the investment options it offers. With an IRA, there is a lot more flexibility. As you learn more about investments over time, you'll want to have more control over where your money goes. Get an IRA, and you can do that. And the tax benefits are awesome. Although traditional and Roth IRAs appear to work in the same way, there are a few key differences you need to be aware of. This should help you decide which one to go for.

For starters, traditional IRAs use pre-tax money, while contributions to a Roth IRA use taxed dollars. Practically speaking, that means you can contribute money to a traditional IRA before your salary hits your bank account. With a Roth IRA, you'll be contributing after it has hit your bank account. That affects the way the traditional and Roth IRAs are taxed upon withdrawal.

When you withdraw money from a traditional IRA at the age of 59 ½, you'll pay taxes on the entire withdrawal amount. That's because you haven't paid taxes on it at any point. With a Roth IRA, you never pay taxes on your contributions since they are post-tax dollars. As for your earnings (or the gains you've made in the account), you'll only pay taxes on those if you **don't** meet the withdrawal requirements (i.e. age 59 ½ and owning the account for five years).

To make life easier for you, I've drawn up a nice table summarizing the advantages and disadvantages of each option.

Roth IRA	Traditional IRA
Advantages	
• Your contributions can be withdrawn tax-free at any time, for any reason, without penalty. • Once you are 59 ½ and have had the account for five years, your earnings can also be withdrawn tax-free.	• Tax benefits are immediate. Your contributions reduce taxable income as and when they are made.
Disadvantages	
• You don't receive any upfront tax benefits for contributing each year. • At higher income levels, contributions are limited. You may not be allowed to contribute to a Roth at all if income is high enough. • Unless you meet certain exceptional criteria, early withdrawals may incur a 10% penalty plus income taxes.	• If you or your spouse have a 401(k) and exceed certain income levels, contributions are limited. • Money withdrawn in retirement is taxed as ordinary income. • Unless you meet certain exceptional criteria, early withdrawals may incur a 10% penalty plus income taxes.

How do you choose between the two? Well, it depends on your individual situation as well as your financial goals. My best advice is to speak to a tax professional if you can. However, below is a checklist of questions you can ask yourself to help make an informed decision.

1. Do you have what the IRS defines as earned income? Only continue if the answer is yes.

2. Are you a high earner? Check income limits for Roth IRA accounts. If your income exceeds a certain amount, you may not be allowed to contribute to a Roth IRA. If that is the case, the decision has been made for you.

3. Do you have a 401(k) retirement plan in place (or does your spouse)? Will your income levels reduce

contributions that are tax deductible? If you don't quality for deductions because of your 401(k) and income, a Roth IRA may well be the best option.

4. Can you think of any reason you might need the money before age 59-1/2? If the answer is yes, a Roth IRA is for you.

5. Are you a disciplined saver? If you get immediate tax benefits, will you use that sensibly or splash the extra cash? (If you've followed the course diligently so far, I'd like to think you've got a solid money-saving mindset.)

6. What sort of tax break do you want? If you think you'll be in a lower tax bracket at the time of retirement, you're better off going for a traditional IRA to take advantage of the tax benefits while your income is high. However, if you think you're likely to be in a higher tax bracket when you retire, it's best to go with a Roth IRA. You won't be taxed on the earnings you receive when you retire, which is a pretty sweet deal.

7. Can you contribute to both? Is that a good idea? I can't answer that for you, but a tax professional can. That is called tax diversification, and those guys are the experts. If you want to be super money-savvy, explore this option.

Investment and Retirement in the UK

In the UK, most people will receive a state pension, which is paid by the government. You are expected to make regular

National Insurance (NI) contributions while working. These are payments deducted from your paycheck that go toward your state pension fund. To qualify for a government pension, you usually need at least ten years of NI contributions. However, the state pension is quite low and unlikely to cover your required expenses in retirement. So it's important to build up your own retirement savings pot over time. To do this, you have 2 options:

1. Workplace or Personal Pension

A workplace pension is the UK equivalent of a 401(k). A percentage of your income is automatically put toward the pension fund each month and your employer may also make contributions on your behalf. Most firms contribute between 3% and 10% of your annual salary each year. If you're self-employed, you can apply for a personal pension. In this case, you choose a pension provider and ask them to invest the funds on your behalf. You can get tax relief on your contributions for both workplace and personal pensions. Always check the gov.uk website for details as there are certain conditions that need to be met.

2. Individual Savings Accounts (ISAs)

ISAs are tax-advantaged accounts. You can invest up to £20,000 in an ISA in the 2020-2021-tax year. There are many different types of ISAs. The two main ones are cash ISAs and Stocks and

Shares ISAs. A cash ISA is essentially a savings account that earns interest. A Stocks and Shares ISA allows you to invest in stocks, investment funds, and bonds, as the name suggests. You do not pay tax on interest on cash in an ISA. You also don't pay tax on income or capital gains from investments in an ISA. *Sweet*, right?

THERE'S AN APP FOR EVERYTHING

Here are the best investment apps for the US:

- *Stash Invest* – There are self-directed and preset portfolios you can invest in. You can choose pre-packaged portfolios of ETFs to suit your goals or you can choose a self-directed account to invest in your choice of ETFs instead. Whatever your choice, remember the strategy you need to follow. It's a great investment learning platform as well.
- *Acorns* – This is best for automated investing. You can transfer amounts periodically and use the round-up feature as described earlier in this book to invest. You can't choose your ETFs, however. The platform does that for you.

These apps have fees, so make a note of them. If they're higher than 0.03% of your principal, open an account with a reputable broker instead, such as Charles Schwab, Vanguard (a financial firm, not a broker), or Fidelity.

If you're living in the UK, here are your best options:

- *Moneyfarm* – Pre-packaged portfolios with minimal fees. Ideal for beginners who don't want too much control over their ETF choices.
- *Wombat* – Wombat has low fees and investment can start from as low as £10. For accounts up to £1,000, there are no account or trading fees.
- *Wealthify* – Offers many choices and is great if you want to target individual market sectors. I don't recommend doing this at first. Start with the broad market and then invest additional cash you might have, over and above your regular contributions.

ACTION PLAN – DAYS 28–30

- Educate yourself more, if needed, with regard to how investments work.
- Discover what your risk tolerance is.
- Compute how much you want to set aside for investing.
- Decide what you will invest in first.
- Choose a retirement account.
- Choose a broker and open an account.

- Start allocating money every month toward your
  investment and retirement accounts. Update your
  budget accordingly.

This chapter was intended to give you a quick introduction to
the world of investing. My next book will be focussed on the
how-to of investing, specifically for students and young adults.
Keep your eyes peeled for that!

CONCLUSION

"Many folks think they aren't good at earning money, when what they don't know is how to use it."

— FRANK A. CLARK

PHEW! We did it. Give yourself a pat on the back. You've taken in a lot of information. This is more financial education than most people get in their lifetime. Most people neglect the importance of a financial education and sign up for mortgages and credit cards without knowing what kind of mess they're getting into. By the time they realize it, it's too late.

You're going to be a lot smarter than that. In fact, the very act of buying this book indicates you're smart and ahead of the game.

Money management appears to be complex because we aren't taught the basics at school, and as soon as we enter the adult world, we're overwhelmed by the wide array of financial and investment products out there, and we don't know what they mean or what to do with them. Hopefully, this book has shown you that personal finance is simple once it's actually broken down and taught to us, like any other subject at school. And all it takes is 30 days of consistent action to get your money under control.

Now, no more visits to the casino, and no more buying lottery tickets! You've seen how simple it is to acquire a million dollars through smart investing over time. By applying the principles in this book and following the action plan, you're more than capable of achieving that. This 30-day program, if followed correctly, will set you up perfectly to reach your financial goals.

If you don't have money to invest, remember that that's the last step. First, take stock of your bills and create a budget. Start establishing an emergency fund, get yourself some insurance, and figure out how your taxes work. Build yourself a strong foundation, and you can grow from there. That's how wealth is made.

Since there is a to-do list at the end of each chapter, I'm not going to repeat what you need to do. What I would like to reiterate are some of the key messages and pieces of advice shared in the book from my personal experiences.

1. Budgeting is literally the foundation upon which your financial success is built. This is not an exaggeration. But it does not mean you can't have fun. I can't stress enough how important it is to have a budget for fun, however small.

2. Use debt wisely. Building a good credit record is important, but don't get sucked in. Credit cards are simply a means to an end.

3. Do what works best for you. When it comes to selecting a budgeting and debt repayment method, you need to make a decision based on your own individual situation. What works for one person might not work for you. The most important thing is not choosing the method but being consistent with it.

4. Don't be a sheep. Be you. Avoid social media if it makes you feel like you need to live a certain way.

5. Think long term. Focus on your financial goals because that is what will allow you to build a happy and fulfilling life.

6. Every little bit helps. Don't think you can't start saving or investing because you don't have hundreds or thousands to spare. Start with whatever you have.

7. Money is a tool. Make it work for you. Not everyone wants millions, but I can say with certainty that everyone craves freedom—freedom of choice and time. Use that to motivate you on this journey.

8. Believe in yourself!

I'm positive this book has given you new insights into money management, along with an action plan you can implement. Please let me know what you think by leaving me a review on Amazon. It helps me understand what I've done well and what I can improve on. The more feedback I get, the more I can help you.

Wishing you the best of luck on your personal finance journey. Let's make some money!

OUR ONLINE COMMUNITY

For support from hundreds of other people on the same journey as you, please join our Facebook group! We share our wins and our struggles. We learn from each other. And we keep each other accountable. I hope to see you there!

Use the link

https://www.facebook.com/groups/30daymoneyschool/

or **scan the QR code:**

If you're more of an Instagrammer, feel free to slide into my DM's. Please **follow me using this link:**

https://instagram.com/30daymoneyschool?r=nametag

or **scan the QR code:**

If you have specific questions to ask on the content of the book, you can book in a FREE 15 minute coaching call with me.

Use this link: https://calendly.com/30daymoneyschool/15min or **scan the QR code:**

REFERENCES

The 7 income streams of millionaires (according to the IRS). *Dividend Real Estate.* https://dividendrealestate.com/7incomestreams/

American consumer debt statistics – Updated 2020. *Credit Summit.* https://www.microcreditsummit.org/american-consumer-debt-statistics/

Annual inflation rates in the United States 1775 – 2019, and the United Kingdom, 1265 – 2019. *MeasuringWorth.* https://www.measuringworth.com/calculators/inflation/

Base, D. (2020, September 23). Should I pay off my student loan early? *Money.* https://www.money.co.uk/guides/should-i-pay-off-my-student-loan-early.htm

Berchick, E. R., Barnett, J. C., & Upton, R. D. (2019, November 8). Health insurance coverage in the United States: 2018. *United States Census Bureau.* https://www.census.gov/library/publications/2019/demo/p60-267.html

Berger, R. (2020, June 17). Small fees have a big impact on your investments. *Forbes Advisor.* https://www.forbes.com/advisor/investing/mutual-fund-investment-fees/

Berry-Johnson, J. (2020, December 10). What is a tax credit vs. tax deduction – Do you know the difference? *Money Crashers.* https://www.moneycrashers.com/what-is-tax-credit-tax-deduction

Bolton, A. (2020, September 17). Warren, Schumer introduce plan for next president to cancel $50,000 in student debt. *The Hill.* https://thehill.com/homenews/senate/516974-warren-schumer-introduce-plan-for-next-president-to-cancel-50000-in-student

Burnette, Margarette. (2021, January 1). 8 best high-yield online savings accounts of 2021. *NerdWallet.* https://www.nerdwallet.com/best/banking/high-yield-online-savings-accounts

Burrows, L. (2020, September 23). Best savings apps in the UK – How to build a savings pot using your smartphone. *Money to the Masses.* https://moneytothemasses.com/banking/best-savings-apps-in-the-uk-how-to-save-money-using-your-smartphone

Caldwell, M. (2020, November 7). 10 budgeting pitfalls and how to avoid them. *The Balance.* https://www.thebalance.com/biggest-budgeting-mistakes-2385610

Carpenter, J. (2019, May 18). Even Harvard is now teaching personal finance. *The Wall Street Journal.* https://www.wsj.com/articles/even-harvard-is-now-teaching-personal-finance-11558171800

Carter, S. M. (2018, May 16). Younger Americans aren't investing in the stock market—researchers think this is why. *CNBC.* https://www.cnbc.com/2018/05/16/gallup-why-younger-americans-arent-investing-in-the-stock-market.html

Consumer Reports: What information furnishers need to know. *Federal Trade Commission.* https://www.ftc.gov/tips-advice/business-center/guidance/consumer-reports-what-information-furnishers-need-know

Cothern, L. (2020, November 25). Emergency funds: Everything you need to know. *Moneyunder30.com.* https://www.moneyunder30.com/emergency-fund

Debt.com's 2020 budgeting survey reveals more Americans than ever are budgeting. (2020, September 23). *Debt.com.* https://www.debt.com/research/best-way-to-budget-2019/

Dilworth, K. (2020, December 23). Average credit card interest rates: Week of December 23, 2020. *Creditcards.com.* https://www.creditcards.com/credit-card-news/rate-report/

El-Sibaie, A. (2019, November 14). 2020 tax brackets. *Tax Foundation.* https://taxfoundation.org/2020-tax-brackets/

Expect high-quality, low-cost ETFs at Vanguard. *Vanguard.* https://investor.vanguard.com/etf/why-vanguard

Fact sheet. *Social Security Administration.* https://www.ssa.gov/news/press/factsheets/basicfact-alt.pdf

Federal Student Aid. https://studentaid.gov/

FOMO fuels American spending. *Charles Schwab.* https://www.aboutschwab.com/modernwealth2019

Friday, L. (2019, May 24). Does the state care more about tax evasion than murder? *Mises Institute.* https://mises.org/wire/does-state-care-more-about-tax-evasion-murder

Goldberg, M. (2020, November 12). How much should you have in savings at each age? *Bankrate.* https://www.bankrate.com/retirement/how-much-do-you-need-in-savings-retirement-emergency-fund/

Goldman, A. Investing 101: Investing basics for beginners. *Wealthsimple.* https://www.wealthsimple.com/en-ca/learn/investing-basics

Gresham, T. What are the primary advantages & disadvantages of index mutual funds? *Zacks.* https://finance.zacks.com/primary-advantages-disadvantages-index-mutual-funds-4030.html

Harvard University. The personal finance workshop. https://www.cnbc.com/2018/05/16/gallup-why-younger-americans-arent-investing-in-the-stock-market.html

Holmes, T. E. (2019, May 6). Americans spend $18,000 per year on non-essentials. *Yahoo! Finance*. https://finance.yahoo.com/news/americans-spend-18-000-per-153406769.html

How to file income taxes in the UK. *Expatica*. https://www.expatica.com/uk/finance/taxes/income-tax-in-the-uk-103165/#taxes

Kiyosaki, R. T. (1998). *Rich dad poor dad*. Warner Books.

Konsko, L., & O'Shea, B. (2018, November 27). No credit vs. bad credit: Which is worse? *NerdWallet*. https://www.nerdwallet.com/article/finance/no-credit-vs-bad-credit-difference

Kurtzleben, D. (2017, April 17). We asked people what they know about taxes. See if you know the answers. *NPR*. https://www.npr.org/2017/04/17/523960808/we-asked-people-what-they-know-about-taxes-see-if-you-know-the-answers

Light, L. (2018, May 20). Why you shouldn't buy life insurance (OK, some may need it). *Forbes*. https://www.forbes.com/sites/lawrencelight/2018/03/20/why-you-shouldnt-buy-life-insurance-ok-some-may-need-it/#1bd0e4701cbb

McCarthy, J. (2020, August 28). The complete guide to health insurance. The Simple Dollar. https://www.thesimpledollar.com/insurance/health/health-insurance-guide/

McKay, F. (2020, June 20). 41 Fascinating life insurance statistics to know in 2020. *SpendMeNot*. https://spendmenot.com/blog/life-insurance-statistics/

Mischel, W. (2015). *The marshmallow test: Understanding self-control and how to master it*. Little, Brown Spark.

Morin, A. (2019, August 20). 7 reasons mental health issues and financial issues tend to go hand-in-hand (and it has nothing to do with the cost of treatment). *Inc.* https://www.inc.com/amy-morin/7-reasons-mental-health-issues-financial-issues-tend-to-go-hand-in-hand-and-it-has-nothing-to-do-with-cost-of-treatment.html#:~:text=One%20study%20found%20that%20individuals,linked%20to%20increased%20financial%20stress.

Orem, T. (2020, November 16). Tax deductions guide and 20 popular breaks for 2020 and 2021. *NerdWallet*. https://www.nerdwallet.com/article/taxes/tax-deductions-tax-breaks

Publication 17 (2020), your federal income tax. *IRS*. https://www.irs.gov/publications/p17

Roth IRA withdrawal rules. *Charles Schwab*. https://www.schwab.com/ira/roth-ira/withdrawal-rules

Royal, J., & O'Shea, A. (2020, October 26). What is the average stock market return? *NerdWallet.* https://www.nerdwallet. com/blog/investing/average-stock-market-return/

Semega, J., Kollar, M., Shrider, E. A., & Creamer, J. (2020, September 15). Income and poverty in the United States: 2019. *United States Census Bureau.* https://www.census.gov/ library/publications/2020/demo/p60-270.html

Sethi, R. (2009). *I will teach you to be rich.* Workman Publishing.

SPIVA U.S. scorecard. *S&P Dow Jones Indices.* https://www. spglobal.com/spdji/en/documents/spiva/spiva-us-year-end-2019.pdf Fspiva

Tierney, S., & Murikami-Fester, A. (2020, December 22). Nerd-Wallet's 4 best money-saving apps. *NerdWallet.* https://www. nerdwallet.com/blog/banking/best-money-saving-apps/

Urosevic, M. (2020, January 1). 21+ American savings statistics to know in June 2020. *SpendMeNot.* https://spendmenot.com/ blog/american-savings-statistics/

Weekly national rates and rate caps. *Federal Deposit Insurance Corporation (FDIC).* https://www.fdic.gov/regulations/ resources/rates/

What is a credit utilization rate? *Experian.* https://www. experian.com/blogs/ask-experian/credit-education/score-basics/credit-utilization-rate/

What is a good or average credit score? *Barclaycard*. https:// www.barclaycard.co.uk/personal/money-matters/credit-scores/what-is-a-good-or-average-credit-score

What's a bond? *CNNMoney*. https://money.cnn.com/ retirement/guide/investing_bonds.moneymag/index3.htm

What's in my FICO scores? *myFICO*. https://www.myfico. com/credit-education/whats-in-your-credit-score

Young, J. (2020, September 3). Before paying off your student loans early, read this. *Credible*. https://www.credible.com/ blog/refinance-student-loans/pay-off-loans-early/

Zemeckis, R. (Director). (1994). *Forrest Gump* [film]. Paramount Pictures.